UNVEILING THE GOSPEL TRUTH BEYOND COLONIAL SHADOWS

ISAAC SITHOLE

UNVEILING
THE
GOSPEL TRUTH
BEYOND COLONIAL SHADOWS

REACH PUBLISHERS

Published by Isaac Sithole using Reach Publishers' services,
P O Box 1384, Wandsbeck, South Africa, 3631

Edited by Melissa Visser for Reach Publishers
Cover designed by Reach Publishers
Website: www.reachpublishers.org
E-mail: reach@reachpublishers.org

ISAAC SITHOLE

nndindeni83@gmail.com

Table of Contents

Acknowledgements

*F*irstly, I dedicate this book to God, my constant source of inspiration and strength throughout the writing process. Without His guidance, wisdom, and grace, this book would not have been possible. I am humbled and grateful for the blessings God has bestowed upon me, and I pray that this book will bring honour and glory to His name. Thank you, God, for your steadfast love, your unwavering support, and your unending grace. This book is a testament to your power and your presence in my life.

Secondly, I would like to dedicate this book to the incredible individuals who helped me bring my ideas to life. Your unwavering support, insightful feedback, and valuable contributions have been instrumental in making this book a reality. Thank you for your dedication, your time, and your unwavering commitment to excellence. This book is a testament to our collaborative effort, and I will be forever grateful for your assistance and guidance.

About the Author

Isaac Sithole was born and raised in the small village of Tsianda, Venda, in Limpopo, South Africa, the fourth child of seven. Life in the village was challenging, with limited resources and few opportunities for success. Despite the hardship, Isaac's family was strong, and they instilled in him a deep sense of faith, hope, and determination.

Growing up, Isaac faced many obstacles, including poverty, tribal and racial discrimination, and a lack of access to quality elementary education. Despite these challenges, he was determined to make a better life for himself and his family. With God's help, he persevered and was able to overcome the odds.

Isaac credits his success to his faith in God and the love and support of his family. After completing his education, he went on to achieve great things in his career, becoming known for his innovative ideas and his commitment to making a difference in his work space and in the lives of others.

Today, Isaac is married to his beautiful wife Finah Omphemetse Sithole and is the proud father of two sons, Mathomo and Triumph Sithole. He remains humble and grateful for the opportunities he has been given and is committed to using his talents and resources to make a positive impact on the world.

Through his life story, Isaac hopes to inspire others to never give up on their dreams, no matter how difficult the circumstances may be. He believes that with faith, determination, and hard work, anything is possible.

Clarifying the Book's Objectives and Audience

Christianity (the Gospel of Christ), Europeanisation, and colonisation are somewhat synonymous in the ears of many, causing Christianity to face massive rejection, especially among previously colonised communities. It is unfortunate that no one has seriously endeavoured to draw the line between these subjects. This book seeks to address the questions many have regarding the origin of Christianity, its purpose, the perceived relationship between the Gospel of Christ and colonisation, and to authenticate the true essence of the gospel.

Focus Audience

This book is intended for a diverse audience, specifically targeting several distinct groups.

First, it aims to reach those who reject the gospel, viewing it as a fallacy and a European tool of control designed to brainwash people for a European agenda.

Second, it speaks to those who see the gospel as just one of many religions to choose from, aiming to demonstrate that the gospel of the Lord Jesus Christ is the ultimate truth for the salvation of all, regardless of ethnic group or other differentiating factors.

Third, the book is directed towards denominations perpetuating incorrect or distorted doctrines and theologies, especially those related to human races, racial hierarchies, and roles thereof.

Fourth, it addresses believers who love God but harbour doubts about the gospel's authenticity as results of external influences and those questioning the gospel's authenticity and eroding their faith.

Fifth, the book is for believers who already know the truth but lack a robust defence for their claims. It serves as a tool to strengthen their convictions.

Sixth, it speaks to believers who are aware of these subject/s or truths but remain silent. It emphasises that their silence acts as a bottleneck, hindering the discipleship the Lord Jesus Christ has instructed the church to carry out. The sooner we are prepared to tackle this topic the earlier we will be able expedite the winning of souls to Christ.

Lastly, it extends to any other group that may have been inadvertently omitted.

Introduction

The authenticity of the Bible has long fuelled intense debates, particularly among intellectuals of non-European descent, asserting that it is a White man's religion primarily created as a tool to facilitate colonisation. This goes to the extent that when one believes in the gospel, they are perceived to be brainwashed, or at least, their intellect becomes questioned. It's understandable when considering the church's avoidance of these questions for the longest time.

It is essential for us, as a Bible-believing community, to acknowledge that those raising these questions and challenging the authenticity of the gospel are well-informed, well-read, and have conducted thorough research. They speak from a place of immense knowledge and evidence. Therefore, providing superficial or emotionally driven responses may prove ineffective. Such responses could give the impression that we are uninformed or possess shallow perspectives, indicating a lack of comprehension regarding what we claim to believe.

Many argue that if Africa had been entirely colonised by Muslims or followers of any other religion, the entire continent would have embraced Islam or that particular religion. This raises the question of whether those of us who have believed in the gospel did so because we found it authentic, or if it was due to external pressure or force, or simply conforming to societal trends.

My perspective has consistently asserted that if the Bible is genuinely true, it must endure rigorous scrutiny. It is crucial to comprehend that genuine faith only takes hold when individuals discover satisfactory answers to their questions — whether through acquiring information or experiencing a supernatural, personal encounter with divinity. Therefore, if we aim to win souls without at least addressing their questions, it will be quite a challenging exercise, unless they have a personal supernatural encounter akin to Saul on his way to Damascus.

In this book, I take the opportunity to expound on the reasons behind my firm conviction that the message of the Bible is authentic. I will share in detail the true and primary purpose of the gospel, which was never colonisation, despite attempts by some groups to co-opt it for colonial rule, unfortunately stigmatising the gospel. I will also discuss in detail these attempts, identify those responsible, and explain the reasoning. I believe our attempt to completely deny that there were attempts to use the Bible to justify slavery is what drives people away because they know such attempts existed. Therefore, we should rather accept this reality and explain where the errors were. Thus, I will provide reasons why we cannot use those attempts as reasons to nullify the true purpose of the gospel. It is important to note that not all European or American missionaries, nor all European citizens or even scientists, were part of that. Many vigorously opposed the idea; it was just a group that had interests. We shall discuss this in depth when we delve deeper later in the book.

Now, it is important to note that if the church is serious about winning souls over, we must provide evidence that demonstrates the inclusivity of the gospel. Therefore, I will also take the time to address some of the major questions raised by the majority of those who reject the gospel. These questions happen to be the very same ill-doctrines that were mostly perpetuated by those who attempted to use the gospel to justify slavery.

I will expose these misconceptions by providing accurate information through the light of God's word. These misconceptions include assertions of curses upon non-Europeans, particularly Africans, being relegated to the bottom of the hierarchy, justification of slavery, and the assertion of these curses as reasons for their economic status. All will be discussed in detail, proving that these assertions have nothing to do with being cursed, as has often been asserted.

I aim to prove that the gospel, in its purest state, has nothing to do with slavery or colonisation but was intended for the liberation and redemption of the world through Christ. How can we expect people to embrace a God who is said to have cursed them? And does it make sense for the same God to call the same people He supposedly hates and still expect them to embrace Him? Otherwise, He will punish them for rejecting Him. Wouldn't it make more sense for them to believe in something that makes them feel human, rather than in a God who constantly reminds them of how cursed they are?

I will support my assertions and convictions through extensive research findings, scientific evidence, archaeological discoveries, historical records, my own personal experiences or encounters, and other forms of evidence, such as insights gained from interviews with credible individuals. All references are listed accordingly for further reading if you wish to do so.

1

Defining the Bible, Decoding Its Essence, and Gospel Foundations

1.1. Defining the Bible: The Book or Text Under Examination

The word 'Bible' finds its roots in the Greek term 'biblia,' meaning 'a book' or 'a scroll.' This collection of inspired texts holds sacred significance for believers in Yeshua, the Messiah, also known as Jesus Christ in English. The name "Jesus" comes from the Greek form of the Hebrew name "Yeshua" or "Yehoshua," which means "Yahweh saves" or "Yahweh is salvation." Yahweh is the name of GOD, which means "the self-existing one". The term "Christ" has its roots in the Greek word "Christos," which translates to "anointed one" or "chosen one." This is where the name 'Christian', meaning followers of Christ, or the anointed ones, comes from. This sacred book is a collection of scrolls from different places, particularly the regions where the characters had encounters with God. The Bible is divided into two main sections: the Old Testament, preceding Jesus Christ's birth, and the New Testament, following His birth, death, and resurrection.

The final version of a modern canonised Protestant Christian Bible comprises 66 books – 39 in the Old Testament and 27 in the New – authored over 1,500 years by 40 diverse writers, including prophets, judges, and disciples. It is important to note that there are other

Bibles, such as Ethiopian Bibles, that contain different numbers of books; however, we will be focusing on the Protestant Bible. The Bible spans various literary genres, including history, poetry, prophecy, letters, and apocalyptic literature. Its richness reflects God's interaction with humanity. The Bible serves as the authoritative spiritual roadmap, guiding with teachings, reproof, correction, and training, as emphasised in 2 Timothy 3:16-17.

For believers from all over the world, the Bible stands as the inspired word of God, capturing divine interactions with humanity throughout history for the benefit of future generations.

1.2. Understanding the Gospel's Purpose, Intent, and Origin

The gospel and the Bible revolve around the covenant that God had with a man called Abraham, the father of faith and the friend of God. It is also important to highlight that before the time of Abraham, there were several other figures mentioned in the Bible who are said to have walked with God and found favour in His sight. Some of these notable individuals include Enoch, who is described in Genesis 5:22-24 as a man who walked faithfully with God and then was taken by God, 'for God took him.' Enoch's close relationship with God is highlighted by the fact that he did not experience death, but was taken directly to be with God. Noah is known for his obedience to God, to the extent that God commanded him to build an ark when God decided to destroy the earth with a flood due to humanity's sins. Genesis 6:9 describes Noah as a righteous man, blameless among the people of his time, who walked faithfully with God.

But, when it comes to Abraham, the Bible informs us that he was the man whom God referred to as a friend, and as a result, God was pleased to the point that He established the everlasting covenant with him, which is the very same covenant we are in today. Now,

Jesus can be traced back to Abraham, and even the three major religions referred to as Christianity, Judaism, and Islam all claim their roots back to the man Abraham.

In the New Testament, a renewed covenant emerges, fulfilling the commitments of the Old Testament and revealing the boundless love of God. Embodied in Jesus Christ, this covenant transcends nationality and ethnicity, extending salvation to all through faith in Jesus Christ. The teachings of the Bible emphasise the inherent sinfulness of humanity, shining a light on the path to redemption for reconciliation with God. Central scriptures, such as Romans 3:23-24, John 3:16, Ephesians 2:8-9, and John 14:6, underscore the essence of the gospel. Grasping its purpose unveils God's redemptive plan, culminating in the New Testament's powerful message of salvation through Jesus Christ.

This gospel, far more than a mere theological concept, offers hope, liberation, freedom, forgiveness, and eternal life to all who embrace it, regardless of their past, origins, race, or background. It stands as a universal source of transformation, welcoming individuals into a divine narrative that transcends the boundaries of human distinction.

## 1.3.	Decoding the Purpose of Bible Canonisation and Assessing Its Importance

In this chapter, our focus shifts to the intricate process of canonising the Bible – an essential undertaking that warrants a dedicated exploration. It's crucial to dispel misconceptions that surround this historical process, often misinterpreted as a European effort to formalise the text for colonial purposes.

Canonisation, in essence, is the formal recognition of specific writings as sacred and authoritative within the Bible. This intricate journey unfolded over centuries, finding its roots in early Christian communities where certain writings were revered as inspired and authoritative. The formal acknowledgement of the canon emerged through extensive discussions, debates, and councils.

It's essential to recognise that, although the process of canonisation was mostly led by the Roman Catholic Church, there were some councils that had stood outside the Roman leading. This process extended beyond Europe, including perspectives from different parts of the world.

Below are the timelines for various councils around the world:

1.   **First Council of Nicaea (325 AD)**
Location: Nicaea (modern-day Iznik, Turkey)
Note: The Council of Nicaea primarily focused on theological issues, particularly the Arian controversy, and did not specifically address the canon of Scripture.

2.   **Council of Laodicea (363-364 AD)**
Location: Laodicea (Asia Minor)
Note: This council produced a list of canonical books for the New Testament.

3.   **Council of Rome (382 AD)**
Location: Rome (Italy)
Note: This council, presided over by Pope Damascus I, compiled a list of canonical books.

4.   **Councils of Carthage (c. 393-419 AD)**
Location: Carthage (North Africa)
Note: Several councils were held in Carthage during this period, discussing and confirming the canon of both the Old and New Testaments.

5.   **Council of Hippo (393 AD)**
Location: Hippo Regius (North Africa)

Note: This council affirmed the canon of both the Old and
            New Testaments.

6.   Orthodox Tewahedo biblical Canon (Approx. 400 AD)

Location: Ethiopia

Note: The Ethiopian Orthodox Tewahedo Church's canon of
            Scripture includes additional books beyond those found
            in the canons of Western Christianity.

7.   Council of Trent (1545-1563 AD)

Location: Trent (in modern-day Italy)

Note: The Council of Trent, convened by the Catholic Church,
            affirmed the traditional canon, and responded to the
            challenges posed by the Protestant Reformation.

The 16th century witnessed the Reformation, a pivotal period when
the Protestant movement arose in reaction to perceived abuse and
doctrinal disagreements within the Catholic Church led by prominent
figures such as Martin Luther and John Calvin. The Reformation sought
to reform various aspects of Christian practice and belief. A significant outcome of the Reformation was the division of Christianity into
diverse Protestant denominations, each with its distinct theological
principles. While theological disparities were paramount, the split
was also influenced by political, social, and cultural factors.

Central to the Reformation was a renewed emphasis on the accessi-
bility of the Bible to all believers. This initiative prompted translations
of the Bible into vernacular languages and a re-evaluation of its con-
tents. Although the Protestant Bible typically comprises 66 books,
decisions regarding the canonisation of these texts were established
earlier in church history. Nonetheless, the Reformation encouraged a
critical review of biblical texts.

In contrast, the Roman Catholic Bible includes additional books known
as the Deuterocanonical books or the Apocrypha. These books, such
as Tobit, Judith, Wisdom of Solomon, Sirach (Ecclesiasticus), Baruch,

and additional portions of Daniel and Esther, were deemed canonical by the Council of Trent in response to the Protestant Reformation. Before the Reformation, debates and variations existed regarding the acceptance of these books.

The discrepancies in the canonisation process during the Reformation led to differences in the number of books between Protestant and Roman Catholic Bibles. While the Protestant Bible contains 66 books, the Roman Catholic Bible includes additional books, totalling 73 books in the canon.

Furthermore, the Ethiopian Orthodox Tewahedo Church maintains a distinct canon that encompasses additional books absent from others. The Ethiopian Orthodox Tewahedo Church acknowledges the Book of Enoch, Jubilees, and additional books of the Maccabees, which are not part of other Christian traditions' canons.

It's worth noting that Christianity as it is known today was challenged and was not entirely the result of a single group. Hence, different councils made distinct decisions, although somewhat aligned. For instance, the Ethiopian Bible differs somewhat from others but still overlaps significantly with the Protestant Bible, conveying the same message of salvation.

1.4. Practical Guidance When Reading the Bible for Better Understanding

Since the Bible has been translated into different versions and languages, it can be challenging to know which version to choose in order to grasp the intended message. Here are some suggestions to help you:

a)   **Choose a reputable translation**: There are many different translations of the Bible, but not all of them are created equal. Some translations are more literal and others are more interpretive. Look for a translation that is widely used and respected by scholars, such as the New International Version (NIV), the King James Version (KJV), the New King James Version (NKJV) or the English Standard Version (ESV) and others.

b) **Read different translations**: Even if you have a preferred translation, it can be helpful to read from other translations as well. Different translations can provide insights into the meaning of the text, and reading multiple translations can help you gain a more complete understanding of the intended message.

c) **Study the historical and cultural context**: Understanding the historical and cultural context in which the Bible was written can also help you better understand the intended message. This can involve researching the political and social climate of the time, as well as the religious beliefs and practices of the people who wrote and received the texts.

d) **Seek guidance from spiritual leaders**: If you belong to a particular community of faith, seek guidance from spiritual leaders, such as pastors or priests, who have studied the Bible in depth and can provide insight pertaining to the intended message.

Most importantly, the best way to grasp the intended message of the Bible within the context it was written is to approach it with an open mind, an open heart, and a willingness to learn. Prayer and meditation can also help you gain insight and understanding through the Spirit of God as you read and study the text.

Examining the Relationship Between Christianity and Colonialism

It is very daunting but also very justifiable to see how the emotions of the majority of non-believers, especially those of African descent, are stirred up or irritated whenever one attempts to preach the gospel to them, revealing unhealed wounds. Therefore, it is important for us to be able to separate weeds from the crop by delving deeper, displaying existing doctrinal errors perpetuated by those who had conflicts of interest, and providing the true essence of the gospel of God in the light of God's word.

Now that we have clarified what Christianity means, as we learnt that it signifies followers of Christ, it is important to delve into defining what colonialism is before we examine their perceived relationship or why they have become intertwined. I am aware that Islam is also one of the religions blamed for participating in the brainwashing of Africans, however, for the purpose of this book, I will confine myself to Christianity as we seek to prove the authenticity of the Gospel of Christ.

Colonialism refers to the establishment, maintenance, and expansion of colonies in one territory by people from another territory. It typically involves political, economic, social, and cultural domination of the colonised territory by the colonial power. Colonialism often involves the exploitation of the colonised land and its resources for the benefit of the colonising country. It can also entail the imposition of the coloniser's laws, customs, and language onto the indigenous population. Overall, colonialism represents a historical and systemic form of oppression and control over colonised peoples and territories.

It is important to note that colonisation dates to ancient times and has occurred among nations seeking to conquer and establish control over other territories. Before the 15th century, colonisation was not primarily driven by considerations of race or colour. Historically, we have observed instances of European countries colonising each other, such as Ancient Greece colonising regions like Southern Italy, Sicily, and parts of Asia Minor, and the Roman Empire expanding its territory to Gaul (modern-day France), Britain, and parts of North Africa. Moreover, Spain colonised parts of Italy, including Sicily and Sardinia, during the Middle Ages, while England and Scotland colonised each other multiple times throughout their history, with periods of dominance and control over various territories.

There were instances where African nations exerted dominance over European territories. For example, during the medieval period, the Moors from North Africa invaded and colonised parts of the Iberian Peninsula, including present-day Spain and Portugal. This colonisation lasted for several centuries, causing a significant cultural and architectural influence. Furthermore, as we have learnt, the Ottoman Empire, with territories in North Africa, launched invasions and colonised parts of Eastern Europe, including areas in the Balkans, Hungary, and Greece. These historical examples illustrate that racial hierarchies or notions of superiority based on race were not significant factors in colonisation until the 15th century.

During this period, colonised nations would occasionally regain their power, toppling another nation to reclaim their independence. According to records, the 15th century marked a peculiar enslavement of non-European groups, particularly Africans, making this instance particularly unique. Africans are still trying to recover after more than 400 years. One might ask why this case differed from others, and whether anything was done differently.

The widely endorsed principle of general empiricism is often advocated for by scholars, researchers, and religious figures. It asserts that an idea can only be deemed empirical when it is substantiated by historical evidence, scientific theories, universal laws, philosophy or authoritative religious scriptures. The narrative had to be backed by any of those fields or both.

Now, during the 15th century, as Spain and Portugal began expanding into new territories during the Age of Discovery, disputes arose between the two powers. The issues were brought to the attention of Pope Alexander VI, and after deliberations the pope issued papal bulls (papal bulls are official decrees issued by the pope, addressing matters of doctrine, governance, and discipline within the Catholic Church and beyond, including papal states) concerning the division of newly discovered lands between Spain and Portugal. One of the most renowned of these bulls was the Treaty of Tordesillas, mediated by Pope Alexander VI and signed on June 7, 1494. This bull divided the newly found lands along a meridian 370 leagues west of the Cape Verde islands (approximately 46°37'W). The purpose of this division was to settle disputes arising from the voyages of Christopher Columbus (sponsored by Spain) and Vasco da Gama (sponsored by Portugal). It is important to note that there had been a close relationship between the Pope and the Emperor. The Pope claimed spiritual authority over all Christians, marking the entire Europe, particularly regions under or previously under Roman rule, while the Emperor sought political legitimacy from the Pope.

The approach followed by this doctrine was used to justify European powers colonising other nations. The premise was that it was biblically correct for a Christian nation (Europe) to colonise non-Christian or Heathen nations, such as Africa and other non-European nations.

   Unveiling the Gospel Truth Beyond Colonial Shadows

This ideology gave rise to other sub-theories such as the "curse of Ham" theory, perpetuated by other Christian denominations, which could be found in the Babylonian Talmud, further placing Africans at the bottom of the hierarchy. This denoted biblical instruction to enslave Africans as they were deemed created for this role, even mocking their skin colour, hair, lips, and even their man-hood as a mark of a curse.

This later paved the way for the rest of the European countries to follow suit until Europe colonised the entire world, with only a few exceptions. Though there was a drive to preach the gospel to convert the locals, unfortunately, we saw some take it to the extreme, exerting severe punitive measures on those who revolted or rejected the gospel. This raised questions about whether the mission was solely to spread the gospel or whether it had other hidden agendas. Unfortunately, no one, particularly the church, has ever endeavoured to provide appropriate answers.

Many African scholars assert the reason behind forced conversion lies in the belief that the converted individual becomes peaceful. Therefore, it was perceived as easier to manage a converted slave. This explains the creation of the Slave Bible, an incomplete version deliberately crafted by removing empowering passages and retaining only those that promoted submission. The Slave Bible is a rare Bible from the 1800s, used by missionaries to convert and educate slaves. This version is currently on display at the Museum of the Bible in Washington, D.C. What's notable about this Bible is not just its rarity, but its content, or rather lack of content. It excludes any portion of text that might inspire rebellion or liberation.

As mentioned before, whenever one needs to validate or drive an idea, it must be supported by historical evidence, scientific theories, universal laws, philosophy or authoritative religious scriptures. Now, we observe that colonial powers and institutions promoted the idea of racial superiority, positioning our European family at the top of the hierarchy and people of African descent at the bottom. Key figures and institutions, including European monarchs, religious leaders, philosophers, and scientists, later contributed to the development and propagation of racial hierarchies through writings, ideologies, and policies. European philosophers such as Immanuel Kant and Johann Friedrich Blumenbach developed racial classification systems that categorised human populations into hierarchical categories based on physical characteristics, eventually leading to the world subliminally accepting this as a way of life.

Now the question remains: Should we nullify Christianity because of this? Were all these acts perpetuated, allowed, or condoned by the Bible? Are there scriptures or verses from the holy Bible that truly support these acts, or were the scriptures simply interpreted out of context?

It is crucial to note that the Pope was not only regarded as the leader of the Roman Catholic Church but also, in essence, the leader in the Papal States. Therefore, understanding Rome's interest in maintaining its political rule, it makes sense that, while there might have been an interest to preach or expand the gospel, there was also the responsibility to play the cards right for their benefits in the political space.

It is important to note that, when the Bible is read within its correct context, one will learn that there are no scriptural bases supporting this position. Instead, the true gospel of the Lord Jesus Christ is for the salvation, liberation, and redemption of all humanity, irrespective of their background or race. In Galatians 3:28, we hear the word of God stating, 'There is neither Jew nor Gentile, neither slave nor free, nor is there male and female, for you are all one in Christ Jesus.' The question remains: Where did the Pope get this from if not from the Bible?

The concept of salvation is based on a person's will and not by compulsion. This is the reason why we have never seen the Lord Jesus Christ or any of His disciples giving people the option of accepting the gospel or losing their lives, and/or property if they deny the gospel.

Such acts, on their own, are antichrist or antibiblical. We even see Jesus Christ saying in the book of John 6:65, 'This is why I told you that no one can come to me unless the Father has enabled them.' This statement came after many of His followers turned away from following Him. In John 6:67, we see Him asking the 12 disciples if they too wanted to return, at which they chose to remain with Him. You can refer to some of the passages below for reference, emphasising the voluntary nature of choosing salvation.

John 3:16 (NIV):
"For God so loved the world that He gave his one and only Son, that whoever believes in Him shall not perish but have eternal life."

Revelation 22:17 (NIV):
"The Spirit and the bride say, 'Come!' And let the one who hears say, 'Come!' Let the one who is thirsty come; and let the one who wishes take the free gift of the water of life."

Romans 10:9 (NIV):
"If you declare with your mouth, 'Jesus is Lord,' and believe in your heart that God raised Him from the dead, you will be saved."

Joshua 24:15 (NIV):
"But if serving the Lord seems undesirable to you, then choose for yourselves this day whom you will serve... But as for me and my household, we will serve the Lord."

Acts 16:31 (NIV):
"They replied, 'Believe in the Lord Jesus, and you will be saved – you and your household.'"

From the article by E.J. Dionne Jr, published in The New York Times on August 14, 1985, we learn that Pope John Paul II apologised to Black Africans for the Church's involvement in slavery. The Pope urged his audience not to perceive these failures as undermining the essence of the Christian message. He stated that, 'The gospel remains a call without equivocation.' This revelation sheds light on the awareness that justifying slavery through scripture was deemed unethical and unbiblical. Again, on Friday, July 10, 2015, Pope Francis is recorded apologising for Catholic crimes against indigenous peoples during the colonisation of the Americas. Again, the question remains: What was the basis for the apology? Was it not because there was an acknowledgement of error? We don't know if the misinterpretation was intentional or an honest mistake, but thank God the error was recognised.

On January 10, 2023, African News shared an article in which the Church of England apologised for its previous links to slavery. The report, released in June 2022, revealed that "the Church Commissioners' endowment had historical ties" to the transatlantic slave trade. In response, Archbishop of Canterbury Justin Welby, the spiritual leader of the Anglican Church, stated, "I am deeply sorry." He emphasised, "The time has come to take action in response to this shameful past."

My perspective on this, as I conclude this chapter after considering the events we have witnessed, is that the Pope's actions (and later other leaders) were not in accordance with scripture. Whether their actions were out of ignorance or deliberate, only God knows. There was a clear attempt to use the Bible as a tool to justify slavery alongside other premises such as science, and later alterations of history were made to strengthen this illusion. This explains why 15th-century slavery or colonisation was so successful and the longest-lasting, to the point where Africa is finding it difficult to recover. This notion has been sublimated even in their education system, media and other platforms, which will be discussed in the following chapters.

We are thankful for other denominations, mostly from the Protestant faith, who have since stood against this idea. It is also comforting that there have been other Popes who have opposed the idea as well, confirming that it was not based on scriptures but error. We see their efforts bearing fruit later. Their success in fighting for the removal of the Slave Bible from public view was testament to their efforts.

Nota Bene: It is important to note that the descendants of the children of Noah, namely Ham, Japheth, and Shem, remains a topic of debate to this day, as the Bible was not very specific on the matter. According to traditional Christian beliefs, Ham is considered the father of Africans, Shem of Asians, and Japheth of Europeans. However, scholars often mix up their descendants, leading to ongoing discussions. For the purpose of this book and to address certain misconceptions, we will adopt the perspective that Ham is the father of Africans, Shem of Asians, and Japheth of Europeans.

3

Exploring Influences on Human Behaviour Beyond Race, Genetics, and Mythical Curses

When analysing human behaviour, it is superficial and deceptive to solely attribute it to race, as this phenomenon extends beyond genetic factors. Research indicates that most behavioural traits are primarily shaped by environmental influences such as the educational system, upbringing or culture, and life experiences. These elements collectively contribute to shaping the human psyche, ultimately resulting in a diverse array of behavioural patterns.

I used to be vigorously puzzled when examining some of the ideas people readily accept as truth – concepts that one would scarcely believe if they engaged in critical thinking. However, my understanding shifted when I encountered the widely endorsed principle of general empiricism, often advocated for by scholars, researchers, and religious figures. This principle asserts that an idea can only be considered empirical when substantiated by historical evidence, scientific theories, universal laws, philosophy or authoritative religious scriptures. It became evident to me why people would embrace such ideologies, considering how the information has been organised and presented to suite the requirement for empirical evidence. This has led to racial profiling, prejudices, and the affected groups being treated inhumanely in many parts of the world, seemingly justifiably

     Unveiling the Gospel Truth Beyond Colonial Shadows

so, since it is written. We see the involvement of geneticists or behavioural geneticists, whose theories align with perverted theories interpretations to validate this hierarchy.

Here, I aim to demonstrate that the behavioural traits observed in disadvantaged populations, particularly Africans, are not the result of genetic flaws stemming from the so-called "Curse of Ham" as mostly misinterpreted. Instead, these traits are linked to psychological impairments resulting from an ugly past. We will examine theories by renowned psychologists to determine whether it can help explain this phenomenon.

It is important to note that Africa was once one of the leading continents when it comes to civilisation. Therefore, one should ask: what went wrong, considering that these people were not inherently disadvantaged? We will delve into this in detail in one of the following chapters.

When making references to behavioural psychology, we learn that information gives rise to ideologies or belief systems, which in turn influence feelings or expectations, culminating in observable behaviours. This explains why the information had to be systematically and intentionally organised.

Abraham Maslow's Hierarchy of Needs provides a lens through which we understand the psychological impact of historical oppression on groups of people or communities, thus undermining the psychological wellbeing and development of the group.

At the foundational level of Maslow's Hierarchy of Needs, Maslow starts by explaining physiological needs, such as access to food, shelter, and basic resources, and the impact thereof. These needs are comparable to the historical challenges faced by Africans and other affected groups due to colonialism and enslavement. Deprivation of such needs likely instilled feelings of insecurity and vulnerability, depriving them of a sense of safety and belonging (a subsequent level of Maslow's hierarchy of needs), ultimately constraining their self-actualisation. Consequently, the legacy of past injustices may have perpetuated a sense of mistrust and division within African communities, impacting their social cohesion and sense of identity. This results in a survival-mode mentality, where people tend to be selfish due to the communal struggle for survival.

African communities, having been subjected to centuries of exploitation and dehumanisation, may struggle to regain a sense of dignity and self-worth. Persistent narratives of inferiority and stereotypes perpetuated by colonial powers can deeply impact the self-esteem of individuals and communities, hindering their ability to assert themselves and fulfil their potential. Moreover, the lack of acknowledgment of past injustices and the erasure of African contributions to civilisation can further exacerbate feelings of marginalisation and inferiority, impeding progress towards self-actualisation and collective empowerment.

Debunking the Fallacy of the Curse of Ham as the Cause of African Calamity

The theory of the curse of Ham, derived by quotation of Genesis 9:25, which reads, "And he said, Cursed be Canaan; a servant of servants shall he be unto his brethren," is one of the foundational theories predominantly used to anchor and justify slavery. If the church is serious about winning souls, especially those of African descent, this serves as the foundation from which to build. The majority are rejecting the gospel because of this perpetual ideology, which is understandable and justifiable when no one is prepared to shine the light. How can one be expected to associate with a God filled with hatred towards them, who can only accept them if they were a slave to others?

I remember one man being asked whether being born again means that the curse will disappear, and his answer was no, it doesn't. Being born again doesn't make you White; it only makes you a repented slave. This statement on its own creates a sense of hopelessness, portraying God as unjust and unforgiving, which is contrary to the God we read about in the Bible. This can also be observed when one visits certain churches where there are seats designated for non-Whites and those designated for our White family. In some churches, Blacks are not welcomed at all, raising questions about whether the group is truly praying to the God of heaven.

Now, when we closely examine Genesis 9:25, we learn that the curse announced by Noah was directed at Ham's son Canaan, not at Ham himself. According to scripture, there was an incident where Ham saw his father naked after Noah had been drinking, and his other brothers discreetly covered their father. Upon waking Noah heard what his son Ham had done and, in anger, Noah cursed Canaan, decreeing that he would be a slave to his other brothers. It also must be noted that Noah couldn't curse Ham because one cannot curse what God has blessed. Remember that God had already blessed Noah and his three sons after the flood. Thus, Noah couldn't reverse God's blessing, leading to the curse directed at Ham's son, Canaan.

It's important to note that Ham had three other sons, namely Cush (Ethiopia), Mizraim (Egypt) and Put (Libya). These three sons were the only ones allocated land on the African continent. There is no record of Canaan (cursed son), the fourth son, being allocated any land in Africa. The only land we know of that was allocated to Canaan is Palestine, where modern Jews and Palestinians coexist.

It is also interesting that although the curse is supposedly on Ham and his descendants, we normally don't hear Egypt included in the curse by those perpetuating the idea. Instead, because of the historical landscape, we see those who propagate the issue claiming that Egypt is White. So, one might wonder whether some of our White families are also descendants of Ham. Why do they want to claim Egypt? Aren't they also supposed to be progenies of a curse? And if Blackness, short hair, and thick lips are the signs of the curse, as alluded to by some literature, then why did all Hamites not turn Black with short hair and thick lips? We all know that Egyptians, Libyans, and even Canaanites, who some believe to be the Palestinians of today, look different. This is only logical if those we know as Egyptians, Libyans, and even Canaanites are not native to those lands, or they are not Hamites at all.

    Unveiling the Gospel Truth Beyond Colonial Shadows

There is an interesting story of Mostafa Hefny, an Egyptian with African features, in the United States. Mostafa Hefny, an Egyptian immigrant, was classified as White despite his African features. This classification stems from the U.S. racial system, which includes five categories: White, Black, or African American, American Indian or Alaskan Native, Asian, and Native Hawaiian or Other Pacific Islander. When Mostafa Hefny inquired about this classification, he was told that he cannot be Egyptian and Black at the same time. Mentioning his Egyptian and Black heritage, he was told that claiming he is both Egyptian and Black would imply that Africa has something to do with civilisation, which he was told cannot be so. Moreover, if he insisted on being classified as Black, he would have lost privileges, leaving him with a choice. His interviews can be found on social media and the internet for those who wish to listen in detail. Does this not expose an underlying agenda?

Was this curse even meant to be eternal? As for the Canaanites, we have already seen the curse manifested even during the Old Testament when God gave their land to Abraham and his descendants. It is important to note that in this instance, the Lord gave the land, and that is recorded, but as for any other invasions happening around the world, those are the will of men and not of God. Additionally, what about Galatians 3:28, which states that there are no longer Jews, Greeks, Gentiles, or slaves, but that we are all one in Christ? Doesn't this scripture revoke the curse?

Today, we live in a world where it is barely possible to find people purely genetically tied to a specific race due to migrations, intermingling, and intermarriages across races. We have almost become the same race, with only surnames left as differentiations and ethnic blocks on birth certificates and passports. However, these are nothing but illusions. If we were to check people's DNA makeup, no one would truly fall under any of those blocks; we are all somehow mixed in varying percentages. And if we were to apply the old American one-drop policy, almost everyone would then be classified as Black.

I know of a White brother who was labelled a "White supremacist," named Craig Cobb, who was behind an initiative to turn a North Dakota town into a "White enclave". He received some shocking news after DNA tests: he was 14% sub-Saharan African and 86% European, and his results were published on the Trisha Goddard Show. What a humbling discovery, isn't it, considering what he was advocating for?

There are many other cases of Black people who appear entirely Black but have an even higher percentage European genetics, not to mention most Blacks in America and other parts of the world. So how does this curse apply? Is it half and half? We see some Black people doing very well in their businesses, even employing White employees, and some in sports. Are they exempted? Just to name a few: Aliko Dangote, $14.2 billion; Abdul Samad Rabiu, $8.2 billion; Robert Smith, $8 billion; Mike Adenuga, $6.1 billion; David Steward, $6 billion; Patrice Motsepe, $2.7 billion; Oprah Winfrey, $2.5 billion; Michael Jordan, $2 billion (2023 statistics). In Africa today, we see an increasing amount of our White brothers and sisters standing at traffic lights begging and some in the parking lots in malls. If this curse is genetic or even spiritual, why this inconsistency? Or are they just Black men hiding in the skin of White men?

With African governments mostly in Black hands, and with policies and systems that work against our White brothers and sisters, making it difficult for them to be employed, we see an increasing number of White families impoverished, with many beginning to live in shacks. Does this not reveal that the prosperity of the group depends on who is running the system? This should not be the case if people live in love and harmony. The way things are going if not corrected swiftly, Maslow's hierarchy theory suggests that our White families may also begin to suffer the same pain and psychological degradation that Black people have endured, something we must fight to prevent because we all deserve to live in a conducive environment, fostering harmony and peace.

     Unveiling the Gospel Truth Beyond Colonial Shadows

Doesn't this expose the fact that the condition of Black Africans is not determined by the terms of the curse or genetics, but environmental factors given that the same conditions can also affect any other group, depending on who is in power or running the government?

Some may ask, 'why is Africa not recovering since power is in their hands now?' The answer is no different from what I have already stated above. These are groups of psychologically impaired people, and their state can only slowly begin to recover after awareness of the past and after having Maslow's basic needs satisfied. Only then, after embracing the fact that they are equal with all humans, will they self-actualise. It is also important to note that though we are no longer in the colonial era, most systems, such as banking and political systems, are still largely controlled from either America or the European Union. This can be seen when they attempt to impose certain ways of living. If challenged, they threaten to withdraw funding. We clearly have not yet reached a place of sovereignty for every nation.

Appearances of Biblical Characters, and God's View on Various Races

$\mathcal{I}$t is important to note that race has no place in the gospel of the Lord Jesus Christ. Rather, it is the heart and character that matter, because salvation transcends ethnic, tribal, racial, and skin colour factors. However, to address the issue at hand, we must talk about the subject because it seems that race has become the most important thing, including to those who have perpetuated their ideas by segregating the people of God.

The race of Jesus and biblical characters has been a subject of interest for a long time. This has resulted in various attempts to portray biblical characters with different racial features, most commonly European. Some may ask why these characters are predominantly depicted as European. The primary reason is that Christianity gained significant momentum and was spread widely as an organised religion by White missionaries during the colonial era, starting in the late 15th century. When looking at countries that were never colonised, like Ethiopia, their depictions of biblical characters resembles themselves. However, these depictions remain localised, since they did not have the opportunity to spread the gospel as extensively as European missionaries. Though we know that some depictions could have been used to perpetuate certain malicious ideologies, I strongly believe that some depictions were innocent. People could only depict characters based on images they could imagine, which often resembled themselves. However, these depictions were unfortunately later co-opted for other agendas.

Genesis 12:1 reads "Now the Lord had said to Abraham: 'Get out of your country, from your family and from your father's house to a land that I will show you.'" We see God asking Abraham to leave his ancestral land and his father's house, promising to guide him to a new land. We know that Abraham hailed from the region of Ur in Chaldea, Mesopotamia, which is in present-day southern Iraq, as referenced in Genesis 11:28 and Nehemiah 9:7, you can google how people from southern Iraq predominantly look. So therefore, in terms of his race, we can already connect the dots, suggesting that he would not have been the way he is predominantly depicted in pictures. This understanding would also apply to Jesus Christ and everyone from the house of Israel, considering that they were all descendants of Abraham.

We can even see the presence of Hamites' ancestry in the lineage that gave birth to Jesus. The same Canaanites who are said to have been cursed by God are married into the very royal lineage that brought forth our Lord and Saviour, Jesus Christ. Namely, Tamar (Matthew 1:3), the Canaanite woman; Rahab (Matthew 1:5), the Canaanite woman; Ruth (Matthew 1:5), the Moabite woman; and Bathsheba (Matthew 1:6), the Hittite woman. So, it seems that God is not as biased towards this race as other people or denominations are towards the "cursed" Hamites.

Various revelations of Jesus, whether through dreams or visions, or near-death experiences depict Him with different complexions in the eyes of the beholders. Various libraries portrayed biblical figures in ancient records with distinct depictions, although the core message remained consistent. Is this not enough to illustrate that God has no vested interest in race? I believe that being God, He would have pre-served the data if race held significant importance.

Some people have been questioning the colour and origin of modern Jews, mostly the Ashkenazi who reside in Israel or Palestine today. Many call them frauds and label them European invaders, while some refer to them as Khazars, suggesting they were converts to Judaism. Some argue that true Hebrews should be Black, pointing to Old Russian Icons from Antique Shops that mostly depict ancient Israelites with dark complexions. Some claim that the darkness of their skins is a result of age affecting the images, while others debate that if discolouration were the cause, even their clothes should have darkened. On the other hand, some argue that they must be more Arab due to the obvious reasons of their origin in Ur, Mesopotamia, leading to widespread confusion.

If I were to answer how true Israelites should look today, I would say that they resemble any race present on earth today. When we read Isaiah 11:12, we learn that He will raise a banner for the nations and gather the exiles of Israel; He will assemble the scattered people of Judah from the four quarters of the earth. It was also prophesied that Israel would be scattered among the nations of the earth because of the people's wickedness (see Leviticus 26:33; Deuteronomy 4:23-27; 28:25, 37, 64.) Based on this scripture, I would not argue that the Ashkenazi Jews are wrong, but I would assert that there are still more Israelites around the world as prophesied in the scriptures, who have possibly intermarried with other races, and that their descendants would be looking exactly like the tribe or race they found in that part of the world. This truth becomes evident when we examine groups such as the Bnei Menashe of India, the Lemba of Zimbabwe and South Africa, the Igbo of Nigeria, the Beta Israel of Ethiopia, and others. Even when comparing them with some amongst well-known Jewish groups, those who conducted the genetic tests confirmed some level of genetic correlation, even though they have different facial features and skin complexions. This means that the Israelites we see today do not entirely represent the full house of Israel, but only a part.

 Unveiling the Gospel Truth Beyond Colonial Shadows

Thanks to my Lemba brothers like Mr Maemu, Mr Tshikomba (Malange) and Mr Sadiki, from Venda in Limpopo, South Africa, who afforded me time for interviews and were willing to share part of their oral history, passed down from generation to generation, not forgetting the documentary by a European explorer who interviewed Samuel Moeti, the then-president of the Lemba Cultural Association. What's more fascinating is that some of these Lemba families, like Malange, Malaka and Selamulele, belong to the Buba tribe, meaning they possess not just a connection to ancient Israel but also a Cohen DNA marker. This marker signifies a priestly lineage, indicating their descent from Aaron. Modern technology also confirms tribe claims. The same is true for other groups that are scattered throughout the earth, as prophesied in the Bible. This means that if we were to bring all their descendants together, Israel would have no base colour, as all tribes and races would be represented. What wisdom of God in trying to unite all human races.

There is also commendable material available for further reading about the claims of other groups identifying as Jewish, beyond the known groups. This material takes the form of books, articles, and YouTube channels. References can be found on the reference page of this book.

Was the Gospel Present in Africa Prior to Missionaries, or Were Missionaries the Sole Conveyors of the Gospel to the Continent?

It's crucial to delve into the state of Africa before the arrival of gospel-bearing missionaries. This exploration aids in determining whether the gospel was entirely foreign or whether it already existed on the continent. It also helps to clarify whether Africans were entirely barbarians or pagan, praying to stones and animals, as many asserted. This does not in any way diminish the commendable work of missionaries.

It's noteworthy that Christianity received official recognition in Aksum (Ethiopia), Eritrea, and Yemen around 330-340 AD, predating the colonial era. It is key to note that the ancient church of Ethiopia had been observing Timkat, a religious festival commemorating the baptism of Jesus, long before the era of European colonialism in Africa, with some asserting that the celebration started before the time recorded by the historians. This celebration has its roots traced back to the 4th century AD according to historians. This significantly predates the initial wave of European colonialism in Africa, which began in the late 15th century, with the Portuguese establishing

    Unveiling the Gospel Truth Beyond Colonial Shadows

colonies, initially in North Africa. The Ethiopian Orthodox Church's deep historical connection to Timkat reveals a rich Christian tradition existing independently of European influences and colonial timelines.

It is also worth noting that while Christian missionaries began arriving in Africa in the early 15th century when Portuguese explorers landed on the continent, widespread missionary activity gained momentum in the 19th century, particularly after the abolition of the transatlantic slave trade. This period saw an increase in missionary efforts aimed at evangelisation and the establishment of Christian institutions across Africa.

Our knowledge regarding who introduced the gospel to Africa or Ethiopia before the arrival of missionaries remains limited. However, Acts 1:15 mentions that around 120 individuals were present in the Upper Room on the day of Pentecost, representing different nations. It is plausible that among these individuals, there were representatives of various races. It is conceivable that the message of the gospel spread from this gathering to people of diverse ethnic backgrounds, including Africa, especially when considering the historical relationship that existed between ancient Israel and Alkebulan translated 'Mother of Mankind', or 'Garden of Eden' currently known by Africa and the geographical proximity between them. Or perhaps through the Ethiopian eunuch – He was a high official in charge of the treasury of the queen of Ethiopia who was converted to Christianity by Philip the Evangelist (Acts 8:26-40).

Observable Influence of Biblical Text (Torah) on African Bantu Culture

The pre-existence of Torah principles or the knowledge of God in Africa is evident in its culture, particularly within the Bantu group. Africa boasts a rich cultural heritage predating colonisation, and intriguingly, significant parallels exist between certain African cultures, especially Bantu culture, and the cultural practices outlined in the Torah (Old Testament). Numerous customs and traditions within Bantu culture remarkably resemble those found in the Bible. These similarities could potentially support the idea that Africans had prior encounters with God, even preceding colonisation.

There are numerous Bantu tribes spread across Africa, making an exhaustive list a challenging endeavour. However, here are some of the more well-known Bantu tribes: Lemba of Zimbabwe and South Africa, Zulu, Xhosa, Swazi, Ndebele, Shona, Tswana, Sotho, Venda, Tsonga, Chewa, Luhya, Kikuyu, Kamba, Ganda, Baganda, Hutu, Tutsi, Congo, Mbundu, Chokwe, Yao, Makua, Luba, Lunda, and Congo. These tribes share a common culture, although with variations due to linguistic and cultural mutations and migrations. The core structure remains similar, and all can be paralleled to those mentioned in the Torah (Old Testament).

It is reasonable to speculate that these traditions were copied or could have originated from the Bible or Torah, as there are no other

   Unveiling the Gospel Truth Beyond Colonial Shadows

apparent sources for their similarities. This suggests that Bantu culture may have had contact with the scriptures long before the arrival of colonisers or missionaries who brought translated versions of the Bible, unless someone tells me that this culture was formed after colonisation or the arrival of missionaries.

Listed below are several examples of African Bantu traditions and practices that are similar to those written in the Bible or Torah:

1. **Circumcision:** The practice of male circumcision in the 8th day is a common tradition among many African ethnic groups, in particular the Bantu people. Similarly, circumcision is also a significant practice in the Bible and is a sign of the covenant between God and Abraham.

2. **Honouring of Ancestors or Respecting Genealogy:** Africans in particular Bantu groups have a cultural practice known as "Izithakazelo" in Zulu, which involves the recitation of ancestral names in a specific order, similar to how the Bible mentions genealogies in the gospels.

3. **Sacrifice of animals:** Animal sacrifice is another practice that is common in both African culture and the Bible. In African tradition, the sacrifice is often offered to appease the *nwali*, UMvelinqangi which they refer to as Most High. Similarly, the Bible mentions several instances where animal sacrifice was used for atonement or as an offering to God. **We thank God for the blood of Jesus that has replaced this practice.**

4. **Hospitality and uBuntu:** The concept of hospitality is highly valued in many African cultures, with guests often being treated with utmost respect and honour. Similarly, the Bible also emphasises the importance of hospitality, with several stories featuring instances of generosity shown to strangers.

5. **Marriage customs:** Many African cultures have unique marriage customs and traditions, such as dowry and bride price

and the procedure thereof. Similarly, the Bible contains several stories and teachings on marriage, including the importance of marital fidelity and the roles and responsibilities of husbands and wives.

6. **Virgin Preservation:** In Africa, particularly among the Bantu, there are ceremonies where girls are checked for virginity, and they receive rewards for maintaining their purity. This is because it's highly encouraged for girls to remain chaste until marriage. The final test is conducted just before she is handed over to her husband. Sometimes, a similar practice involves the husband being given something like a butternut shell (calabash), symbolising that the girl being given to him is still a virgin. We can observe a parallel to this in the Bible, where a cloth is used during a woman's initial encounter with her husband to see if there's any bloodstain. If the test is failed, the consequences could include death.

7. **Marrying One's Brother's Widow:** In Bantu culture, it is common to marry one's deceased brother's widow to continue his lineage, which is a practice also found in the Bible.

8. **Belief in a single God:** A significant number of Bantu people hold a belief in a single God who they believe resides in heaven.

9. **Polygamy:** In the Bantu group, it is common for a man to marry more than one wife, especially kings, chiefs or the wealthy, which can be paralleled to monarchy in the bible.

10. **Shaving of Hair in the Case of Death in the Family:** Shaving one's head as a sign of mourning or bereavement was a cultural practice that symbolised grief and loss. We also see the same practice in the biblical text.

11. **Dietary Restrictions:** Some Bantu communities have dietary restrictions similar to those found in Hebrew dietary laws

   Unveiling the Gospel Truth Beyond Colonial Shadows

(kashrut). For example, in certain Bantu cultures, there are restrictions on consuming certain animals like those mentioned in the Torah, and certain foods are considered taboo.

12. **Ceremonial & Combat Dance and Music:** Both Bantu and Hebrew traditions involve music and dance as integral parts of religious and cultural celebrations, sometimes even as combative instruments. Interestingly, the Venda people have what they refer to as Ngomalungundu, a drum they would strike and dance to, to honour Nwali, their God, whom they refer to as the Heavenly God. When they dance while playing the instrument, they believe it allows them to gain power over their enemies. Is it coincidental that this resembles what the Israelites did, even around Jericho?

Many parallels can be drawn, but I believe those mentioned above are sufficient to draw the picture.

Believing in one God is a fundamental aspect of African Bantu culture. While there might be individuals who incorporate other beliefs, the core and foundational belief remains centred on a single God. The Nguni/Zulu people of South Africa refer to their God as UMvelinqangi, which is a Zulu word for "The original being", "the first to appear" or "the Most High," considered the source of all that has been, that is, and all that ever will be. They refer to him as Spirit, or someone who cannot be seen by optical eyes. Likewise, the Sotho people refer to their God as Modimo or Ramasedi, meaning "God" or *Rama* means "God" and *sedi* means "light" which may be translated as "The Shining One". The Vhavenda believed that Nwali/Raluvhimba was a universal God and that He was the only creator of mankind on earth. They therefore referred to Him as Musika Vhathu or Mutumbuka Vhathu (creator of mankind). The Shona and Kalanga people also refer to Him as Nwari, which sounds much closer to the Venda God, and the list goes on.

While they may not have much knowledge of the trinity structure, they do have a strong belief in the one most high who resides in heaven. Many of them have shared stories of their ancestors' encounters with God while praying to Him in the mountains. These sacred mountains and caves still exist today and hold great significance to their communities.

I want to clarify that although my ancestry is distant Ngoni, I grew up among the Venda, Lemba (also known as African Hebrews due to their culture), Northern Sothos and Tsonga speaking people, and therefore, most of my first-hand experiences and observations come from their culture which is similar to our Ngoni brethren with minor variances due to lingual mutation and migrations.

The Significant Roles Played by Africans (Hamites) in the Bible

The contribution of the Hamites, or Africans as they are believed to be, is often overlooked compared to the louder echoes of the curse narrative. In this discussion, we will categorise Ham's descendants based on the geographical areas where they are believed to have settled, as Ham is considered the progenitor of all African people. It should be emphasised that while African nations were not directly referred to as "Africa" or "Alkebulan," they are mentioned in the Bible using names like Egypt, Ethiopia, Libya, Cush, Put, Sheba, Havilah, and Midian, Canaan (Palestine) before God gave the land to ancient Israel.

To clear up any confusion, it is worth noting that "Alkebu-lan" is the oldest known name for Africa. It is believed to have originated from Arabic and means "The Land of the Blacks" or "Mother of Mankind." Some scholars suggest that it meant "garden of Eden".

Below are several individuals mentioned in the Bible who were/-are Hamites (African) and their respective contributions.

1. **Tamar** – She played a significant role in the genealogy of Jesus (Matthew 1:3). *("Judah the father of Perez and Zerah, whose mother was Tamar, Perez the father of Hezron, Hezron the father of Ram.")* Perez is mentioned in the genealogy of Jesus.

2.   **Bathsheba** – She was the wife of Uriah the Hittite and later became the wife of King David, and later the mother of King Salomon making her a part of the lineage of Jesus (Matthew 1:6).

3.   **Rahab** – Ancestor of King David and Jesus, as mentioned in the genealogy of Jesus in Matthew 1:5. *(Rahab is named as the mother of Boaz. Boaz, in turn, is the great-grandfather of King David.)*

4.   **Moses' Cushite wife** – She is believed to have been from the Hamitic nation of Cush (Numbers 12:1-16).

5.   **Simon of Cyrene** – He was the man who was forced to help Jesus carry his cross (Mark 15:21).

6.   **Ebed-Melech** – He was an Ethiopian man who helped rescue the prophet Jeremiah from a cistern (Jeremiah 38:7-13).

7.   **The Queen of Sheba** – She was a wealthy queen who visited King Solomon and was impressed by his wisdom (1 Kings 10:1-13).

8.   **The Ethiopian eunuch** – He was a high official in charge of the treasury of the queen of Ethiopia who was converted to Christianity by Philip the Evangelist (Acts 8:26-40).

9.   **Hagar** – She was Sarah's Egyptian slave and the mother of Abraham's first son, Ishmael (Genesis 16:1-16).

10.   **Asenath** – The wife of Joseph and the mother of Manasseh and Ephraim (Genesis 41:45, 50-52). This implies that the descendants of Manasseh and Ephraim had Hamitic ancestry, suggesting that other Israelites also have Hamitic ancestry.

Isn't it interesting that we don't hear about this from those who propagate the curse of Ham? It's possible that if they learnt about this, assuming they haven't already, it could be a humbling experience for

    Unveiling the Gospel Truth Beyond Colonial Shadows

them, especially since these Hamites didn't just contribute passively; some of them were even part of the lineage of the Lord Jesus Christ. They were fortunate that the 'one-drop blood rule' had not yet been introduced by then; if it had, Hamites might have had the right to claim the entire lineage, including our Lord Jesus Christ.

God has consistently shown affection to these people. If He truly wished for them to perish, how can one explain the ongoing phenomenon of manna falling in the southern part of Angola? Isn't this a demonstration of God's love for His people? The Namba Adventist Station in Southern Angola has been receiving manna twice a week (Wed & Fri) since as far back as 1945, not sure if have changed today. It is also recorded that when the members of this Church are not in good standing, they receive bitter manna (red colour one). The same sustenance He provided for His chosen nation is now being given to those whom some groups claim are cursed and abandoned by God.

Exploring Africa's Influence on Global Civilisations and Challenging Claims of Inferiority

The belief that the curse of Ham and inferior genetics (illusion) caused Black people to suffer throughout history is a misguided interpretation of the biblical story. It is important to note that if this curse was indeed spiritual or ingrained in their DNA by God, it should have started manifesting from then onwards. However, we see ancient Africans as one of the pillars of ancient global civilisation, which was unfortunately interrupted when colonial powers took over.

It is important to note that when colonial powers take over, they impose the colonisers' laws, customs, language, and government or economic systems onto the indigenous population. These systems work in favour of the colonial powers and against the indigenous population, dictating what resources or education the colonised people can access. This often results in training individuals only to the extent that they are deemed suitable to serve as slaves. In the words of Willie Lynch (1712), if you maintain this system for three generations, you will have produced a group of people who are intellectually weak, to the point where they cannot even stand on their own, affecting them for hundreds of years, even after regaining their independence. Is this not what we see in Africa today?

   Unveiling the Gospel Truth Beyond Colonial Shadows

It is also documented that ancient Greek scholars, often considered among the first civilised Europeans, exchanged knowledge with ancient Africans through trade and various interactions. Some of the notable individuals who have written about the idea of Greeks learning in Africa include the Senegalese historian and scholar Cheikh Anta Diop, as well as writings by Herodotus, a Greek historian and geographer.

Prior to European colonisation of Africa, several notable and advanced civilisations existed on the continent, including the Kingdom of Kush, the Kingdom of Axum, the Mali Empire, and the Songhai Empire, among many others that will be discussed. These civilisations had distinct cultures, languages, and achievements in areas such as mathematics, astronomy, art, literature, and architecture. Despite attempts to plunder evidence and destroy libraries and other valuable resources that could attest to this reality, we can be grateful that proof and evidence remain in the libraries at Timbuktu and in some artifacts certain European countries are now beginning to voluntarily return to the continent.

It's also crucial to note that many of the artifacts mentioned earlier were crafted from gold, bronze, brass, and various minerals. These materials serve as evidence that people of African descent were already engaged in mining and metal processing pre-colonisation.

I know there has always been an ongoing debate seeking to separate Egypt from the rest of Africa. Now, for the sake of this discussion, we will reference the fact that Egypt, which originated from Mizraim, is descended from Ham, whom we already agreed are the progenitors of Africans, unless it means that some of groups amongst our White brothers are also descendants of Ham. So, it is important that we do not lose that train of thought.

It is also important that we note the genetic diversity observed among people in North Africa reflects the complex history and interactions of various populations in the region over thousands of years.

This means that the current population might not entirely or accurately represent the indigenous population of old, as it is a result of the intermixing of different races, considering the history of the land. How they looked remains speculation to this day, but at least we can conclude, based on biblical accounts, that they were Hamites, children of Ham, the father of Mizraim, later translated to Egypt. Ham, which means burnt, hot, or warm – many also say it means Black – is where the assumption of him being the progenitor of dark races originates.

9.1. World Civilisation and Their Timelines

It's crucial to understand that every continent has played a role in shaping civilisation in its own unique way, drawing from its strengths and evolving at different times. Some nations learnt from others, while some built upon the achievements of their predecessors, pushing boundaries further. Below are timelines of civilisations to appreciate the contributions made by each continent toward global civilisation.

9.1.1. Africa Civilisation

Ancient Civilisations
a)   Ancient Egypt (c. 3100 BCE – 332 BCE)
b)   Nubia (c. 2000 BCE – 350 CE)
c)   Carthage (c. 9th century BCE – 146 BCE)
d)   Axum (c. 100 CE – 940 CE)

Medieval Kingdoms and Empires:
a)   Ghana Empire (c. 8th century – 13th century)
b)   Mali Empire (c. 1235 – 1600)
c)   Songhai Empire (c. 15th century – 1591)
d)   Great Zimbabwe (c. 11th century – 15th century)

Colonial Period:
a)   All seized in the 15th century due to colonisation.

     Unveiling the Gospel Truth Beyond Colonial Shadows

9.1.2.   *Asian Civilisation*

Ancient Civilisations

a)   Mesopotamia (c. 3500 BCE – 539 BCE)

b)   Indus Valley Civilisation (c. 3300 BCE – 1300 BCE)

c)   Ancient China (c. 2100 BCE – 221 BCE)

Classical and Medieval Period

a)   Han Dynasty in China (206 BCE – 220 CE)

b)   Tang Dynasty in China (618 – 907)

c)   Islamic Golden Age (8th century – 14th century)

d)   Mongol Empire (c. 1206 – 1368)

Colonial Period

a)   All seized in the 15th century onwards with European powers establishing colonies in Asia.

9.1.3.   *European Civilisations*

Ancient Civilisations

a)   Ancient Greece (c. 8th century BCE – 146 BCE)

b)   Roman Empire (c. 27 BCE – 476 CE)

Medieval Period

a)   Fall of the Roman Empire (476 CE)

b)   Byzantine Empire (c. 330 – 1453)

c)   Holy Roman Empire (800 – 1806)

Renaissance

a)   14th to 17th centuries

Colonial Period

15th century onwards, with explorations, conquests, and colonisation by European powers.

9.2.   Several Ancient Wonders in Africa Predating Colonisation

There are many ancient wonders in Africa that predate colonisation, demonstrating the rich and advanced civilisations on the continent. Here are a few examples:

1.   **Great Zimbabwe:** An ancient city built in the 11th century, Great Zimbabwe is a remarkable archaeological site known for its impressive stone structures, including the Great Enclosure and the Hill Complex. It challenges the stereotype of Africa as a primitive and uncivilised continent.

2.   **Adam's Calendar:** Located in Mpumalanga, South Africa, Adam's Calendar is a megalithic site believed to be the oldest man-made structure on Earth. It consists of standing stones arranged in a circular pattern, possibly serving as an ancient astronomical calendar.

3.   **The Pyramids of Meroe:** Located in present-day Sudan, the pyramids of Meroe are a collection of ancient pyramids built by the Kingdom of Kush. These pyramids are evidence of the advanced civilisation that existed in the region long before European colonisation.

4.   **Axum Obelisks:** Found in the ancient city of Axum in present-day Ethiopia, these obelisks are towering stone pillars that were erected as funerary markers for ancient tombs. They showcase the architectural and engineering skills of the Axumite civilisation.

5.   **Benin City Walls:** The Benin City Walls in present-day Nigeria are a series of earthworks and walls built to fortify the city of Benin. The sophisticated construction of these walls challenges the notion of African societies as lacking in organisational and engineering skills.

 Unveiling the Gospel Truth Beyond Colonial Shadows

These wonders demonstrate the depth of African history and challenge stereotypes that portray Africa as a continent devoid of advanced civilisations before European colonisation. They highlight the rich cultural, architectural, and technological heritage of various African societies.

9.3. Numerous Mines and Industries Operational Prior to Colonisation

Below are numerous mines and industries that were already operational and played a significant role in the continent's economy and cultural development before colonialism. Examples include:

1. **Gold Mines:** Africa had rich gold deposits, and gold mining was widespread across the continent. Prominent gold mining regions included the Kingdom of Ghana (present-day Mali and Burkina Faso), the Kingdom of Mali, the Akan states (present-day Ghana), the Kingdom of Zimbabwe, and various regions in West Africa. You will recall that Mansa Musa of Mali was once the richest man on the planet, owing to the gold reserves he possessed.

2. **Iron Ore:** The oldest mine in Swaziland is the Ngwenya Mine, known for its iron ore deposits. The mine is located near the western border of Eswatini (formerly Swaziland) and has a history dating back thousands of years. Archaeological evidence suggests that iron ore mining and smelting activities were carried out at Ngwenya as early as the Stone Age.

3. **Salt Mines:** Salt mining was a crucial industry in West Africa. The salt mines of the Sahara, particularly in the regions of present-day Mauritania and Mali, supplied salt to neighbouring regions, and the Trans-Saharan trade routes facilitated the exchange of salt for other commodities.

4. **Copper and Iron Mines:** Copper mining and smelting were prevalent in regions such as Nubia (present-day Sudan), the Great Lakes region, and parts of Central Africa. Ironworking was also widespread, with iron mines and smelting operations found in various parts of the continent.

5. **Stone Quarrying:** African civilisations engaged in stone quarrying to obtain materials for construction, sculptures, and tools. Notable stone quarrying sites include the ancient Egyptian quarries in the Nile Valley, which provided limestone and granite for monumental architecture.

6. **Textile and Weaving Industries:** Textile production and weaving were well-established industries in many African societies. Cotton cultivation and weaving flourished in regions such as West Africa (notably the Mali Empire), East Africa (Swahili city-states), and the Kingdom of Kongo.

7. **Pottery and Ceramics:** Pottery making was a prevalent craft throughout Africa. Skilled artisans produced functional and decorative pottery using different techniques and materials. Notable pottery traditions include the Nok culture in present-day Nigeria and the pottery of the Great Zimbabwe civilisation.

8. **Salted Fish Industry:** Along the West African coastline, a thriving industry centred around the production and trade of salted fish developed. This industry involved fishing, processing, and preserving the fish by salting them, providing a valuable commodity for intercontinental trade.

9. **Trading Networks:** Africa had extensive trade networks that connected various regions and facilitated the exchange of goods. The Trans-Saharan trade route, which linked West Africa with North Africa and the Mediterranean, and the Swahili coast trade network in East Africa were prominent examples of vibrant commercial activities.

     Unveiling the Gospel Truth Beyond Colonial Shadows

9.4. African Innovators Often Overlooked in Textbooks

It is equally important to acknowledge and recognise inventions created by Black individuals but often omitted from historical accounts. The selective recording of history was influenced by an agenda that propagated the notion of Black inferiority. Here are some noteworthy inventions that should not be overlooked:

1. **Sarah E. Goode (C. 1850-1905):** She invented the folding cabinet bed, a space-saving furniture piece that could be transformed from a desk to a bed.

2. **Lewis Howard Latimer (1848-1928):** Latimer played a crucial role in the development of the incandescent light bulb. He improved the carbon filament used in the bulb, making it more durable and efficient.

3. **Garrett Morgan (1877-1963):** Morgan invented the three-position traffic signal, which included a warning sign to halt traffic, allowing for safer intersections.

4. **Marie Van Brittan Brown (1922-1999):** She created the home security system, which included a closed-circuit television system with remote monitoring and a two-way communication feature.

5. **Granville T. Woods (1856-1910):** Woods invented various electrical devices and systems, including the multiplex telegraph, which allowed multiple messages to be transmitted simultaneously over a single wire.

6. **Dr Patricia Bath (1942-2019):** Dr Bath invented the Laserphaco Probe, a medical device used for cataract treatment, revolutionising the field of ophthalmology.

7. **Mark Dean:** He played a pivotal role in the development of the personal computer. Dean co-invented the ISA bus, which enabled multiple peripheral devices to be connected to a computer.

8.   **Madam C.J. Walker (1867-1919):** Walker, an entrepreneur and philanthropist, developed a successful line of hair care products specifically designed for Black women. She became one of the first self-made female millionaires in the United States.

9.   **George Washington Carver (1860s-1943):** Carver was a prominent agricultural scientist and inventor. He is known for his extensive research on crop rotation and the many practical uses he discovered for peanuts, sweet potatoes, and soybeans.

10. **Otis Boykin (1920-1982):** Boykin invented various electronic devices and made significant contributions to the field of resistor technology. His innovations played a crucial role in the development of numerous electronic applications, including pacemakers, computers, and guided missile systems.

11. **Shirley Ann Jackson:** Dr Jackson became the first African American woman to earn a doctorate from the Massachusetts Institute of Technology (MIT). She made groundbreaking discoveries in the field of theoretical physics and conducted influential research in telecommunications.

12. **Lonnie G. Johnson:** Johnson is an engineer and inventor who is best known for creating the Super Soaker, a popular and highly successful water gun toy that revolutionised the water toy industry.

13. **Thomas Fuller (1608-1661):** was an extraordinary individual, often regarded as a genius for his extensive contributions to literature and history.

Examining Perceived Contradictions in the Biblical Text

After conducting extensive research and engaging in in-depth study, my conclusion is that most of the alleged discrepancies in the Bible are not significant; rather, they stem from minor errors caused by the following key factors:

1. **Copyist Errors:** Over time, certain ancient manuscripts have encountered copyist errors that led to inconsistencies.

2. **Chronological Difficulties:** The variations in time measuring and dating methods among Babylonians, Greeks, Egyptians, and Romans have contributed to some chronological challenges.

3. **Ambiguity in Language:** Similar to English, some Greek-to-Hebrew words have multiple meanings. Importantly, these linguistic nuances haven't altered the Bible's correct message or context.

It's essential to recognise that these issues, often labelled as discrepancies, do not significantly impact the overall accuracy and integrity of the biblical text.

10.1 Most Perceived Discrepancies in Bible Text

Below are some of the most highlighted issues considered as discrepancies. I have provided explanations that aim to reconcile them:

1. **Creation Accounts:** Genesis 1 and 2 present differing viewpoints on creation, not conflicting tales. Genesis 1 outlines a structured, seven-day universe formation, highlighting God's majestic order. In contrast, Genesis 2 zooms in on human creation and Eden's formation. While divergent in emphasis and detail, they don't present a strict chronology. Rather, they harmonise, providing varied insights into the main creation narrative.

2. **Accounts of Jesus' Genealogy:** The gospels of Matthew and Luke portray distinct genealogies for Jesus. In Matthew's account, the lineage traces through Abraham and King David, emphasising Jesus' royal and Jewish heritage. This genealogy highlights key figures and historical milestones, anchoring Jesus within the context of Israel's history. On the other hand, Luke's genealogy traces through Mary, Jesus' mother, and extends further back to Adam, underlining Jesus' connection to all of humanity. Luke's focus is more inclusive and universal, aligning Jesus with the entirety of human existence. These differing genealogies reflect each gospel's unique theological and narrative intentions, emphasising Jesus' role as both the rightful heir of Israel's promises and the universal Saviour.

3. **Discrepancies in Numbers:** Numbers in the Bible sometimes exhibit inconsistencies (Exodus, Numbers, and Deuteronomy). For example, the count of Israelites departing Egypt varies among different books due to diverse counting methods or viewpoints. Ancient texts frequently utilised symbolic or rounded numbers for literary impact rather than strict accuracy.

4. **Differences in Resurrection Narratives:** The four gospels depict diverse details about Jesus' resurrection. For

example, the count and identity of women at the tomb and the sequence of events differ. These variations stem from the authors' intentions, focus, and their sources of information. They emphasise distinct facets of the resurrection story rather than suggesting contradictions.

5.   **The Age of King Jehoiachin:** In 2 Kings 24:8, Jehoiachin's age at becoming king is listed as 18, while 2 Chronicles 36:9 states 8 years old. This seeming contradiction could be clarified by varying methods of age calculation. It's plausible that the age in 2 Chronicles indicates Jehoiachin's co-regency with his father before his independent kingship.

6.   **The Order of Jesus' Temptations:** The gospels of Matthew, Mark, and Luke all depict the account of Jesus' temptations in the wilderness. While the core narrative remains unchanged, there is a difference in the order of temptations presented in these gospels. This variation can be understood because of the gospel authors organising the events to align with their unique theological and literary goals, rather than indicating a contradiction in the actual chronological sequence of events. Each author chose to emphasise specific aspects of the temptations and their significance within their broader narrative, contributing to the overall theological message of their gospel. This diversity in presentation reflects the writers' intentions and does not necessarily undermine the integrity of the story itself.

7.   **Judas' Death:** The accounts of Judas Iscariot's death in Matthew 27:5 and Acts 1:18-19 vary. Matthew indicates Judas hanged himself, while Acts reports he fell headlong, and his body burst open. These accounts could align if we speculate that after Judas hanged himself, the rope or branch may have broken, causing his body to fall, resulting in a gruesome impact that disfigured his body.

8. **The Resurrection Appearance Locations:** The gospels depict varying locations for Jesus' post-resurrection appearances. Matthew mentions Galilee, whereas Luke and John concentrate on Jerusalem. These differences arise from the distinct perspectives and emphases of the gospel authors. They highlighted specific appearances based on their theological and narrative intentions.

9. **The Denial of Peter:** The gospel accounts differ in their portrayal of Peter's denial of Jesus. Matthew, Mark, and Luke all record a rooster's crow following Peter's third denial, whereas John's gospel mentions the rooster crowing twice. This variation underscores John's specific intention to offer additional detail, accentuating the fulfilment of Jesus' prediction regarding Peter's denial. The double mention of the rooster's crow in John's account serves to emphasise the accuracy of Jesus' prophetic words and underscores the gravity of Peter's actions. These distinctions among the gospel narratives reflect each author's unique perspective and the way they chose to emphasise certain aspects of the story without necessarily implying contradictions.

10. **The Last Words of Jesus:** The gospels offer varying depictions of Jesus' final words on the cross. For example, Matthew and Mark include the cry, "My God, my God, why have you forsaken me?" In contrast, Luke records Jesus saying, "Father, into your hands, I commit my spirit." These differences can be viewed as distinct perspectives or summaries of Jesus' concluding moments on the cross.

11. **The Timing of Jesus' Cleansing of the Temple:** The Synoptic Gospels – Matthew, Mark, and Luke – place the account of Jesus' temple cleansing toward the end of His ministry, whereas John's gospel positions it at the beginning. This discrepancy arises from the gospel writers' emphasis on thematic

   Unveiling the Gospel Truth Beyond Colonial Shadows

organisation rather than strict adherence to chronological order. Each author crafted their gospel to convey specific theological and narrative messages. The Synoptic Gospels highlight Jesus' confrontation with religious authorities closer to His crucifixion, while John uses the temple incident to introduce Jesus' ministry and establish His authority. These variations in the placement of events demonstrate the writers' intent to illuminate different aspects of Jesus' life and teachings rather than indicating contradictions in the sequence of events.

12. **Where Cain Found His Wife:** One of the most debated aspects concerning the narrative of the biblical account revolves around the question of where Cain found his wife. The answer is relatively straightforward: he married his sister. It is crucial to recognise that, until the time of Moses, people were permitted to marry their close siblings. As we delve into the narrative, we discover that Abraham, for instance, had wed his sister Sarah.

It's noteworthy that, according to Genesis (Genesis 5:4), the Bible instructs us that Adam and Eve had borne other children. To explore this further, please refer to Genesis 5:4.

Key Reasons I Embraced the Gospel as Unquestionable Truth

I am a naturally curious and critical person, as well as a qualified engineer. This combination has fostered in me a tendency to question and analyse ideas rather than accepting them without scrutiny. It is essential to acknowledge that my beliefs, including those related to the Bible, have undergone rigorous examination and testing. They are not solely influenced by emotional impulses but have been subject to thorough scrutiny and evaluation.

In the upcoming sections, I will provide a comprehensive account of how I reached the conviction that the Bible and the gospel are true. I will share detailed information obtained from various sources, such as research studies, scientific findings, archaeological evidence, personal testimonies, and spiritual encounters from my own life.

It is essential to emphasise that the information I present can be verified through credible sources, such as books, the internet, and other reliable references. While I can assure you of the authenticity of my personal testimonies, they cannot be independently and easily verified unless individual witnesses of the occurrences are interviewed. I can also make an effort to provide their contact information if anyone wishes to verify. It is also important to note that I have no ulterior motives for sharing these testimonies. I personally gain nothing from people accepting the gospel. The ultimate benefit is for individuals to encounter God for the salvation of their souls. Therefore, there is no reason for me to deceive or fabricate information.

Through my journey of learning, I have realised that an effective methodology for fact-checking begins with the initial assumption that the idea or document being evaluated could potentially be false. This approach helps eliminate biases that may arise from preconceived notions or placing the idea or book in question on a pedestal. It involves subjecting the idea or document to a rigorous process of scrutiny, irrespective of its esteemed reputation. Rather than relying solely on its perceived validity based on reputation, it is crucial to treat it like any other source and subject it to thorough examination. This was precisely the process I underwent when evaluating the Bible, subjecting it to thorough examination before confirming its veracity.

In my methodology for validating and examining the authenticity of the Bible, I consider various factors beyond a biblical account when evaluating an idea or determining the validity of a hypothesis. I have therefore followed the recommended scholarly approaches by considering the following factors:

1. **Empirical evidence:** Look for objective and verifiable evidence that supports the idea or hypothesis. This can include scientific research, experiments, observations, and data analysis.

2. **Consistency with existing knowledge:** Assess whether the idea aligns with established theories, principles, and laws in relevant fields of study. Consistency with well-established knowledge increases the likelihood of validity.

3. **Reproducibility:** Determine if the idea or hypothesis can be tested and replicated by others. If multiple independent experiments or studies yield similar results, it strengthens the validity of the hypothesis.

4.   **Peer review and scholarly consensus:** Consider the opinions and evaluations of experts in the relevant field. Peer-reviewed research papers and consensus among scholars provide additional support for the validity of an idea or hypothesis.

5.   **Logical coherence:** Evaluate the internal consistency and logical coherence of the idea. It should be free from contradictions and should follow a rational line of reasoning.

6.   **Predictive power:** Assess whether the idea or hypothesis can make accurate predictions about future observations or events. If the predictions derived from the hypothesis consistently match the outcomes, it adds credibility to its validity.

7.   **Cross-disciplinary support:** Examine if the idea finds support or corroboration from different disciplines or areas of knowledge. Consensus or convergence across multiple disciplines strengthens the validity of the hypothesis.

Considering these factors, one can assess the validity of an idea or hypothesis beyond relying solely on a biblical account. However, it would be unfair not to acknowledge my personal experience. Despite being raised in a Christian family, I reached a point where I started questioning my faith. This led me to pause and embark on a sincere exploration to uncover the genuine truth and authenticity of the Bible and the gospel. My aim was to discern whether they were truly valid or merely a deceptive construct driven by hidden agendas.

I invite you to explore my personal journey, aiming to inspire your own quest for truth. I'll begin by sharing my compiled personal experiences and testimonies, along with fulfilled biblical prophecies that affirm the Bible's authenticity, supported by archaeological, biological, scientific evidence, and more.

11.1 A Compilation of Personal Experiences and Testimonies

Born and raised as the fourth of seven siblings in Tsianda, a Venda village in Limpopo, South Africa, I was nurtured in a family guided by devout parents who instilled seeds of faith in me from a young age. Following the wisdom of King Solomon in Proverbs 22:6, my parents diligently steered me onto the righteous path, imparting enduring values. Their unwavering dedication laid the foundation for my steadfast faith, sustaining me through moments of questioning and examination of the gospel's authenticity.

I feel fortunate to have encountered extraordinary supernatural events within and around my life. It's essential to note that my exceptional Christian parents, though my father has passed away, demonstrated a faith that transcended mere words. Their lives were characterised by unwavering faith, accompanied by tangible demonstrations of divine power. I personally witnessed them bringing things into reality through spoken words, praying for the healing of the sick, and engaging in various extraordinary acts in the name of Jesus Christ, guided by their deep devotion.

I would like to share the experiences that have significantly contributed to strengthening my faith in the completed work of Calvary.

11.1.1 *Early Experiences During My Pre-Adolescent Stage*

First Experience: I have a vivid memory of a blessed day when I was around eight or nine years old. It was a Saturday, and as the rain poured down heavily, accompanied by terrible hail, my father was away attending a conference hosted by our affiliated denomination, IAG (International Assemblies of God). Inside our rondavel house, my mother stood up, gazing through the window, concern etched on her face since she thought the rain would disturb the ongoing crusade. In that moment, she boldly and unwaveringly declared in our native language, "In the name of the Lord Jesus Christ, I rebuke the spirit of thunder, rain, and hail to cease." Miraculously, everything came to a sudden halt. Filled with excitement, I, as a young boy, rushed out to the street, proudly announcing that it was my mother who had brought about the cessation of the rain.

Second Experience: There was a child born with a condition characterised by excessive salivation (hypersalivation), difficulty in swallowing (dysphagia), and speaking (dysarthria). The Church organised a prayer for healing, and miraculously, the boy was completely restored. This remarkable experience left a lasting impression on my father, who often shared the story, highlighting how the boy eventually became a police officer and married. Although I hadn't met the man in question, I believed my father. This wasn't the first miraculous act I had ever witnessed or heard of, whether performed by him or by the church using the name of Jesus the Messiah.

Third Experience: One of my brothers fell ill, and my mother took him to the clinic. Upon their arrival, the nurses sadly declared that he had already passed away. However, for some reason, my mother firmly believed that her child was not dead and decided to take him back home. It was a challenging journey as she carried him on her back, and the towel she used as support failed since his body was malleable. This caught the attention of people along the way, as they witnessed her determination to bring her child home, despite the lack of a vehicle and the distance to the clinic.

Now, through her unwavering faith and continuous intercession, my mother experienced a miraculous moment. By the grace of God, the child came back to life, defying all expectations and proving the power in the name of Jesus Christ.

Fourth Experience: I have a vivid memory from my teenage years when I was around 15 years old. Like any typical teenager, I felt the temptation to engage in activities that my peers were involved in. On one particular evening, I arrived home a bit later than usual, only to find my parents waiting for me in the living room. I could sense the suspicion in my father's eyes as he wondered where I had been. In that moment, something extraordinary happened.

I distinctly recall hearing what I can only describe as a voice speaking directly to me. It compelled me to step outside the house and find solace under the nearby avocado tree. The voice continued, cautioning me about the potential dangers of the path I was about to embark on. It alerted me of the consequences that awaited. Alongside those warnings, there was also a promise. The voice assured me that if I chose to abandon those pursuits, the Lord would become my Father, and I would have nothing to worry about.

Remarkably, everything the Lord promised me that night has been gradually unfolding with each passing day.

Firth Experience: I was born with a unique condition where it appeared that I had missing hair on the front part of my head. As I reached the age of around twelve, it started to progress, giving the impression that I was going bald. It was an incredibly humiliating experience for a young boy to go through. Other children would mock me with hurtful names. Each time I looked in the mirror, it seemed to worsen, robbing me of joy and confidence.

However, at the tender age of twelve, a thought echoed in my mind: Could God grow hair on the areas where I had none, so that I could look like any other child? Without hesitation, I answered with a resounding "yes, I believe." My brother had a large mirror in his room clamped on the wall. I would go in there almost every day, stand in front of the mirror and command my hair to grow, expressing my desire for hairstyles like the popular German and Police cuts trending at the time.

To my amazement, the very same children who used to mock my baldness were the first to notice that hair was sprouting where it hadn't been before. I had to go see for myself, and indeed, my hair was being gradually restored even better than before the mysterious loss. This miraculous transformation not only restored my hair but also my confidence. It is the reason I can proudly wear a stylish hairstyle today.

Sixth Experience: I was seated with my late father, who served as a pastor and was chosen by God for the ministry of deliverance and miracles. We were having lunch one afternoon at his new stand we had been building when we noticed a quarrel between two gentlemen nearby. It appeared that our neighbour had hired one of the men to install his roof but had failed to fulfil his payment obligation. As a result, the disgruntled worker left in anger.

After some time, we observed a whirlwind forming in the direction from which the gentlemen had departed. It gained strength and momentum as it approached our vicinity. Just as it was about to pass through by my father's stand, he raised his hand, directing it to change course in Jesus' name. Astonishingly, the whirlwind obeyed his command, altering its path on a new route towards the target house with the roof installed by the gentleman in question. We watched in awe as the roof of the house was lifted as though carried by a multitude of unseen forces.

Once the task was completed, the whirlwind retraced, following the same route it had taken when it first approached us. This extraordinary occurrence made me realise the undeniable power present in the name of Jesus, capable of even commanding magic or evil to submit and obey.

Seventh Experience: My grandfather was a spiritualist and herbalist who relied on his bones for spiritual insight. He was widely respected, sought after for consultations, and had discovered a method to influence events. As a young man, I recall witnessing peculiar occurrences whenever I visited his rondavel house. Despite his son being a minister of the Word of God, my grandfather continued practicing these spiritual rituals.

In the early '90s, as his time on earth neared its end, my grandfather urgently summoned my father, while lying on his deathbed. Many assumed he wanted to pass on his spiritualist mantle, as is customary in such traditions. However, my grandfather had a different mantle to bestow, the mantle of the gospel. He sat my father down and revealed previously undisclosed information, emphasising that my father must never pursue traditional spiritualism but remain devoted to his role as a minister of the gospel. He urged my father to dedicate himself wholeheartedly to God's calling, emphasising that Yeshua (Jesus) is the sole path to salvation.

After their heartfelt conversation, my grandfather asked his son to lead him through the sinner's prayer, to Christ. Just as my father departed, he received a call from the hospital notifying him that my grandfather had passed away.

Allow me to highlight a crucial aspect of this testimony. The individual in question was not an ordinary or average person; rather, he possessed a heightened awareness of the spiritual realm. This same person, who had deep insights into the spiritual world, encouraged his son to wholeheartedly devote himself to God's calling, emphasising that salvation could only be found through Yeshua (Jesus).

For those who may harbour doubts regarding the existence of Christ or question the legitimacy of the gospel, it is possible that you have not yet encountered a truly profound spiritual encounter. However, this individual understood the potential consequences of leaving this world without surrendering his life to Christ. Recognising this, he made a deliberate choice to embrace Christ, with the intention of bringing glory to God.

11.1.2   *My Experiences During Tertiary Education*

It would be unjust to overlook the experiences I had while at university; it would seem that I had reached the pinnacle of faith. I could only attribute it to the foundation laid by my parents and my own personal journey as a young man. It is important to recognise that my faith was also shaped by the challenging circumstances I encountered during my university years, where I faced difficulties in accessing necessities that other students had readily available. These circumstances significantly impacted my first year of tertiary studies.

It became evident to me that there were limitations to what my parents could assist me with, and I had to place my reliance on someone far greater and more powerful than them – God. These circumstances led me to recognise the need for a deeper connection with Him and reinforced my trust in His providence.

Like our previous discussion, I would like to share a selection of experiences from my university days that have strengthened my conviction in the authenticity of the gospel.

First Experience: After the glorious break at home when it was time to return to the university, I became aware that my father lacked the necessary funds to cover all the expenses. In earnest, I prayed to God in the name of Jesus, asking for assistance with my payments. To my astonishment, upon my arrival in Vanderbijlpark, the owner of the flats informed me that I had already paid for that month. Although I couldn't ascertain how or when it happened, I knew in my heart that it was a provision from God. Gratefully, I expressed my thanks to Him for this provision.

Upon realising the power inherent in the name of the Lord Jesus Christ, I made a conscious decision to leverage this authority and ask for things I lacked. Below, I will share some of the experiences that unfolded as a result.

Second Experience: I found myself in a situation where I didn't have the required book for Thermodynamics, which was priced around R300, or less if purchased second hand. Unfortunately, I lacked the funds to acquire even a second-hand copy. I distinctly remember praying for the provision of this book on a Monday, as classes had

     Unveiling the Gospel Truth Beyond Colonial Shadows

already started, with the upcoming week being a crucial time (Test Week). By Wednesday, I reminded God of my request, hoping that Friday would not arrive without a book in my possession.

On Friday morning, as I sat in the assembly area, seeking warmth from the sun, I fervently prayed once again, reminding God of my need. Approximately an hour later, a gentleman from QwaQwa who was also a student in the university approached me, carrying a bag filled with books. He informed me that a fellow student had purchased all the books but was unable to obtain approval from the dean for all the subjects. As a result, he decided to give the book to me. Curiously, when I inquired about the person who had initially purchased the book, the gentleman did not disclose their identity.

Reflecting on this experience, I was compelled to acknowledge the undeniable power present in the name of Jesus. How can I ever deny the truth of the gospel when such occurrences manifest before me?

Third Experience: Having witnessed the tangible evidence of answered prayers and the incredible power inherent in the name of Jesus, I found myself praying for a bursary during the break in my second year. I explicitly conveyed to God that I was unwilling to return to the university without a bursary, and I requested a sign to affirm His provision. To my amazement, within a span of three days, I received a phone call from a company inviting me for a bursary interview. This ultimately led to a bursary that not only covered my school expenses but also alleviated financial burdens.

There are countless instances that I can solely attribute to the power of God. However, if I were to include all of them in this book, it would become excessively large and potentially overwhelming for readers.

11.1.3   *Sharing My Post-University Experiences*

Even after leaving the university, I continued to witness inexplicable miracles that defy logical explanation. At times, it felt like a dream, and I can only attribute these experiences to invoking the power in the name of the Lord Jesus Christ. In this book, I will share a select few post-university experiences, mindful of the content's volume. However, I firmly believe that these chosen experiences will shed light on why I am deeply convinced of the authenticity of the Gospel of the Lord Yeshua Hamashiach.

It is often said that a person blessed with the experience of God is not easily swayed by someone with mere arguments. Therefore, I invite you to explore my personal experiences shared below, with the hope that they will be a source of blessing to you.

First Experience: In 2004, during my experimental training at Goldfields, I would often sit in a specific spot on the commuter transport. One afternoon, as I returned from work, I distinctly heard a voice suggesting I change my seating location. Surprisingly, there was an incident that very afternoon, resulting in severe damage to the exact spot I usually occupied. Those seated nearby were injured. How could I possibly deny the power in the name of Jesus Christ after witnessing such an experience?

Second Experience: In 2009, I undertook a business trip from the small town of Ermelo in Mpumalanga, South Africa, back to Johannesburg. As I made my way back, the sun was setting, and darkness enveloped the landscape as I drove my VW Polo. The road I travelled on was frequently congested with trucks transporting coal to the Power Generating Station.

While driving behind a truck for some time, I noticed a chance to overtake. Unfortunately, I was unaware that there were two trucks travelling side by side, and by the time I realised it, it was too late. I found myself confronted with an oncoming vehicle.

The details of what transpired next are unclear to me. All I remember is that somehow, miraculously, I ended up in front of the two trucks. In the aftermath of this incident, I was left in a state of shock, trying to comprehend what had just happened. I spent several months

   Unveiling the Gospel Truth Beyond Colonial Shadows

questioning myself and seeking answers from various spiritual leaders, hoping that God would reveal the truth about that fateful day. However, the circumstances surrounding the event remain a mystery to this day.

Third Experience: Around 2010, while driving the same vehicle mentioned earlier, I was on a journey from Witbank to Ermelo in the province of Mpumalanga, South Africa. My vehicle experienced a malfunction that caused the gears to disengage, resulting in extremely high engine revs whenever I pressed the accelerator. Despite my efforts, I could only manage a speed of around 30 kilometres per hour on the freeway. To alert other drivers of my predicament, I activated the hazard indicators and continued driving in the yellow lane until I reached the off-ramp.

As soon as I exited the freeway, the gears reengaged, and the high revs disappeared. I contemplated taking the car to a VW Service Centre for inspection, but I decided to continue my journey while monitoring the situation. I resumed my route by on-ramping onto the freeway again. After driving for a few kilometres, I came across a massive accident involving multiple vehicles. Reflecting on the incident, I realised that the time lost from my journey may have prevented me from being involved in the accident.

As someone who regularly prays for travelling mercies before embarking on trips, how could I possibly doubt the existence of a God who listened to my prayers and ensured my safety on that day?

To my astonishment, my vehicle never experienced the same issue again. Even when I explained the incident to the VW Service Centre later, they couldn't provide an explanation for what had happened. It became evident to me that this was nothing short of the hand of the Lord at work.

There are numerous other inexplicable experiences that even non-believers can recognise as unmistakably divine interventions. When faced with such clear evidence, how can I possibly doubt the authenticity of God's presence and power?

11.2 Fulfilled Biblical Prophecies Validating the Authenticity of the Bible

In this book, I have listed 16 biblical prophecies that substantiate the divinity and authenticity of the Bible, a book written approximately 3,500 years ago. The remarkable nature of these prophecies, which could not have been known without divine revelation, attests to the undeniable significance of the Bible. Although the exact dates of authorship for each book may vary, the earliest texts are estimated to have been written around 3,500 years ago, further highlighting the profound foresight contained within its pages. Contained within this compilation are astonishing examples of prophetic evidence that will leave one's mind truly astounded.

1. **The Restoration of Israel (Ezekiel 37:21-22):** This prophecy predicts the regathering of the scattered people of Israel to their homeland, which was realised with the formation of the modern state of Israel in 1948. While there are many individuals of Israeli heritage believed to still be spread worldwide, hidden in different races, the significant establishment of the state stands as a crucial milestone.

2. **Global Communication (Revelation 11:9-10):** This verse illustrates how individuals worldwide will witness and share news about major events, aligning with today's global media coverage and instant communication.

   Unveiling the Gospel Truth Beyond Colonial Shadows

3. **Wars and Rumours of Wars (Matthew 24:6-7):** Jesus predicts ongoing conflicts and rumours of wars, and the prevalence of armed conflicts and geopolitical tensions in the modern world reflects this prophecy's fulfilment.

4. **False Prophets and Deception (Matthew 24:11):** Jesus' caution regarding the emergence of misleading prophets who deceive many is becoming increasingly evident in today's proliferation of cults, false teachings, and misleading ideologies.

5. **Famine and Natural Disasters (Matthew 24:7):** Jesus speaks of a time when there will be famine and natural disasters. The prevalence of food crises, droughts, hurricanes, earthquakes, and other calamities in the modern world aligns with this prophecy.

6. **Spread of the Gospel (Matthew 24:14):** Jesus foretells the global spread of the gospel before the end. The widespread dissemination of Christian teachings and missionary efforts to all corners of the world is evidence of this prophecy.

7. **Unrest and Persecution of Christians (Matthew 24:9):** Jesus predicts that His followers will face persecution and hatred. The ongoing persecution of Christians in various parts of the world affirms this prophecy is fulfilled.

8. **Increase in Lawlessness (Matthew 24:12):** Jesus warns that lawlessness will prevail in the last days. The rise in crime rates, moral decay, and societal unrest in the modern world point to the fulfilment of this prophecy.

9. **Increase in Travel Speed (Daniel 12:4):** Daniel's prophecy speaks of a time when people will run to and from, suggesting a significant advancement in transportation. The modern era's high-speed travel methods, such as airplanes and trains, fulfil this prophecy.

10. **Rise of Apostasy (2 Thessalonians 2:3-4):** This prophecy foretells a widespread departure from the true faith in the last days. The modern era witnesses a decline in biblical adherence and the rise of secularism.

11. **Globalisation of Trade (Revelation 18:11-13):** The Bible predicts a global market system, mentioning specific goods and commodities. The modern world's interconnectedness through international trade and the prominence of the mentioned products confirms this prophecy.

12. **Rise of Artificial Intelligence (Revelation 13:15):** This verse alludes to the creation of an image that can speak. Artificial intelligence and the development of interactive virtual assistants has shown rapid advancement.

13. **One-World Government (Revelation 13:7):** The Bible anticipates a time when political power will be consolidated under a global authority. The modern push for global governance and the formation of international organisations hints toward this prophecy.

14. **Mark of the Beast (Revelation 13:16-17):** This prophecy speaks of a mark that will be required for economic transactions. The modern development of cashless payment systems, biometric identification, and implantable microchips raises parallels to this. Though it is believed that the full implementation will happen after the rupture of the church, signs already hint to this end.

15. **Increase in Earthquakes (Matthew 24:7):** Jesus mentions that earthquakes will occur in various places. There has been a rising frequency and intensity of earthquakes in recent times.

16. **Hedonism and Disregard for Traditional Values (2 Timothy 3:1-5):** This passage describes a time when people will be

Unveiling the Gospel Truth Beyond Colonial Shadows

lovers of self, ungrateful, unholy, and without self-control. The moral decay, hedonism, and disregard for traditional values has become prevalent in the modern world.

The alignment of biblical prophecies with modern world events strongly affirms the divine and authentic nature of the Word of God. This analysis sheds light on the connection between these prophecies and the Bible's truth, reinforcing its authenticity.

11.3 Non-Christian Historical References Substantiating the Authenticity of the Gospel

While non-Christian historical references to the events described in the gospels are relatively limited, there are a few notable examples that provide some external confirmation of the authenticity of the bible or gospel. Here are a few:

1. **Flavius Josephus:** Josephus, a Jewish historian of the first century, made references to Jesus and early Christianity in his writings, particularly in "Antiquities of the Jews." The key passages include the mention of Jesus, John the Baptist, and James, Jesus' brother.

2. **Tacitus**: Cornelius Tacitus, a Roman historian of the first century, mentioned Jesus and the early Christian movement in his work "Annals." In a passage discussing the Great Fire of Rome in AD 64, Tacitus refers to "Christus" (Christ) who suffered under Pontius Pilate and the subsequent persecution of Christians by Emperor Nero.

3. **Pliny the Younger**: Pliny the Younger, a Roman governor and writer of the early second century, corresponded with Emperor Trajan regarding the persecution of Christians. Pliny's letters provide insights into early Christian practices and beliefs, though they do not directly reference events in the gospels.

4. **Suetonius**: Suetonius, a Roman historian of the second century, mentioned Jesus and early Christians in his work "Lives of the Twelve Caesars." In his biography of Emperor Claudius, he refers to the expulsion of Jews from Rome due to disturbances instigated by "Chrestus" (possibly a misspelling of Christus) and their association with him.

5. **Mara Bar-Serapion**: A Syrian philosopher from the first or second century, Mara Bar-Serapion, wrote a letter to his son in which he mentions the Jews' execution of their "wise king." While the specific identification of this figure as Jesus is debated, it is a possible reference to him.

6. **Lucian of Samosata**: Lucian, a Greek satirist of the second century, wrote a work called "The Death of Peregrinus," which includes a passing reference to Jesus and the Christians. Although primarily satire, it reflects the existence of early Christian belief and the crucifixion of Jesus.

7. **Celsus:** Celsus was a second-century Greek philosopher who wrote a critical work called "On the True Doctrine" against Christianity. While his work aimed to refute Christian beliefs, it indirectly provides insights into the early Christian movement and its claims.

8. **Thallus:** Thallus, a historian from the first century, wrote a work on the Eastern Mediterranean history, now lost, but referenced by later Christian authors. Julius Africanus, a Christian historian of the third century, quoted Thallus in his writings, noting Thallus' attempt to explain the darkness that occurred during the crucifixion of Jesus.

9. **Tertullian:** This early theologian lived in North Africa (present-day Tunisia) during the second and third centuries. Tertullian wrote extensively in defence of Christianity and addressed various theological and ethical issues. While he doesn't provide

direct historical references to the gospel events, his writings contribute to our understanding of early Christian beliefs and practices in the African context.

These non-Christian historical references, while limited, provide some external confirmation of the existence of Jesus and early Christian communities.

11.4 Archaeological Evidence Substantiating the Authenticity of the Gospel

Archaeology has contributed to our understanding of the historical context in which the events of the gospels took place. While archaeological findings cannot directly confirm specific details or events described in the gospels, they can provide broader contextual support.

11.4.1. Renowned Biblical Archaeologist

Below are some scholars and archaeologists who have made significant contributions in providing archaeological evidence that supports the authenticity and historical reliability of the Bible.

1.   **William F. Albright (1891-1971):** William F. Albright, a renowned biblical archaeologist, made significant contributions to validate the historical accuracy of the Bible through archaeological findings. His excavations and research helped confirm the existence of various biblical cities and figures. Albright's work in the ancient Near East provided substantial evidence that supported the narratives presented in the Bible. He emphasised the correlation between archaeology and biblical texts, strengthening the case for the historical reliability of the Bible.

2.   **Merrill F. Unger (1909-1980):** Merrill F. Unger, another respected archaeologist, contributed to the validation of the

Bible's authenticity through his scholarly work. His expertise in Semitic languages and his archaeological research supported the historical and cultural context of biblical narratives. Unger's comprehensive approach involved linguistic, historical, and archaeological evidence, which collectively reinforced the credibility of the Bible's accounts.

3. **Millar Burrows (1889-1980):** Millar Burrows, an influential archaeologist and biblical scholar, conducted research that highlighted the harmony between archaeological discoveries and biblical descriptions. His work at sites like Qumran, where the Dead Sea Scrolls were discovered, shed light on the historical background of biblical texts. Burrows' expertise in ancient manuscripts and artifacts provided valuable insights into the preservation and accuracy of biblical records.

11.4.2. Other Archaeological Findings

Below are some archaeological findings presented for your consideration, serving as evidence supporting the accuracy of biblical texts.

1. **The Pool of Bethesda:** The Pool of Bethesda, mentioned in the Gospel of John (John 5:2-9), was believed to be a healing pool in Jerusalem. In the 19th century, archaeological excavations uncovered a site near the Sheep Gate with a pool that matched the biblical description. This discovery supports the existence of the pool and lends credibility to the gospel account.

2. **The Pilate Stone:** In 1961, an inscribed stone known as the Pilate Stone was discovered in Caesarea Maritima, an ancient Roman city. The inscription mentions Pontius Pilate, the Roman governor who presided over the trial and crucifixion of Jesus, confirming the historical existence of this figure mentioned in the gospels.

3. **The Caiaphas Ossuary:** In 1990, an ossuary (bone box) was discovered in Jerusalem bearing the inscription "Joseph, son

of Caiaphas." Caiaphas was the high priest during the time of Jesus, and the ossuary likely contained the remains of his son. This discovery provides archaeological evidence for the existence of Caiaphas and his prominence in the events surrounding Jesus' trial.

4.   **Sepphoris:** Sepphoris, located near Nazareth, is an archaeological site that was a significant city during the first century. Excavations have revealed a prosperous cosmopolitan city with evidence of Roman influence. Some scholars speculate that Jesus and his family might have had connections to Sepphoris, and it provides insights into the socio-cultural context of the time.

5.   **The Synagogue at Capernaum:** Capernaum, a village near the Sea of Galilee, is mentioned numerous times in the gospels as a place where Jesus taught and performed miracles. Excavations have uncovered the remains of a first-century synagogue at the site, supporting the presence of a Jewish community during Jesus' time.

6.   **The Nazareth Inscription:** Discovered in the late 19th century, the Nazareth Inscription is a marble tablet with an edict issued by the Roman Emperor Claudius around 41-54 AD. Although not directly related to the events of the gospels, the inscription serves as evidence for the practice of Roman crucifixion, which aligns with the crucifixion of Jesus described in the gospels.

7.   **The Magdala Synagogue:** In 2009, an archaeological excavation at Magdala, a town in Galilee associated with Mary Magdalene, uncovered a first-century synagogue. This finding provides insights into the religious and social context of the time, supporting the presence of a Jewish community and the likelihood of Jesus teaching in synagogues.

8.   **The Pilgrimage Road:** The discovery of the Pilgrimage Road in Jerusalem, announced in 2019, sheds light on the processional route used by Jewish pilgrims during the time of Jesus. The road connects the Pool of Siloam with the Temple Mount, offering potential insights into the routes Jesus and his followers might have taken during key events described in the gospels.

9.   **The James Ossuary:** The James Ossuary, a bone box inscribed with the Aramaic inscription "James, son of Joseph, brother of Jesus," gained attention in 2002. While there have been debates and controversies surrounding its authenticity, its potential connection to Jesus' family, specifically the James mentioned in the gospels, has generated interest among scholars.

10. **The House of Peter in Capernaum:** Archaeological excavations in Capernaum have revealed a house believed to be the residence of the apostle Peter. The house shows evidence of early Christian veneration and has been associated with various gospel accounts, such as the healing of Peter's mother-in-law (Mark 1:29-31).

11. **Noah's Boat:** Naval engineers found that the proportions or dimensions utilised in the construction of Noah's Ark, as described in Genesis 6:15, are ideal for ensuring the stability of this barge-type watercraft, especially for navigating turbulent waters without propulsion. Is this not perplexing, especially when done by people who had no knowledge of naval architecture or marine engineering?

11.4.3. *Scientific Acknowledgement of Biblical Validity: Insights from Prominent Minds*

Below are quotes from prominent scientists emphasising their acknowledgement of the compatibility between science and faith, and some even expressing their conviction in the presence of a divine creator as depicted in the Bible.

1. **Werner von Braun, the astronomer and former director of NASA:** "It is as difficult for me to understand a scientist who does not acknowledge the presence of a superior rationality behind the existence of the universe as it is to comprehend a theologian who would deny the advances of science."

2. **Sir Isaac Newton:** "I find more sure marks of authenticity in the Bible than in any profane history whatsoever."

3. **Blaise Pascal:** "The knowledge of God is very far from the proofs of God."

4. **Albert Einstein:** "Science without religion is lame, religion without science is blind."

5. **Max Planck:** "Religion and natural science are fighting a joint battle in an incessant, never-relaxing crusade against scepticism and dogmatism, against disbelief and against superstition, and the rallying cry in this crusade has always been, and always will be, 'On to God!'"

6. **Michael Faraday:** "In no sense can the separation of science and religion be said to be advocated by a true knowledge of nature. On the contrary, our great object is to show that, as far as science can teach us anything, they are mutually dependent on each other."

7. **James Clerk Maxwell:** "The Bible is true, and science is true, and therefore each, if truly read, but proves the truth of the other."

8.   **Francis Collins:** "I have found there is a wonderful harmony in the complementary truths of science and faith. The God of the Bible is also the God of the genome."

9.   **William Thomson (Lord Kelvin):** "Overwhelmingly strong proofs of intelligent and benevolent design lie around us. The atheistic idea is so nonsensical that I cannot put it into words."

11.5. Alignment with Universal, Scientific, and Philosophical Laws

The Bible and God have been subjects of controversy for centuries. Many people question the origins, authenticity, and purpose of the Bible, with some asserting it is a tool used by elites to control humanity. But is that true? Perhaps this provides an opportunity to delve a bit deeper!

When reading the Bible in context, it can be regarded as more of an OEM manual – a life manual inspired by God the Creator for all humanity. Another point to note is that philosophy, science, and other natural laws are simply humanity's attempts to discover the fabric of this great design. If done correctly, they should align with the scriptures, otherwise, they become fallacies. Thanks to technology, this alignment is becoming clearer, all pointing to the undeniable existence of one great God, the God of the Bible.

Below are examples of some of the laws that can be traced back to the scriptures amongst many others:

I.   **Cause and Effect**

❖ **Scientific Principle**: Every effect has a cause. This is a fundamental concept in physics and other sciences.

❖ **Biblical Scripture**: "In the beginning, God created the heavens and the earth" (Genesis 1:1). This scripture implies a cause (God) for the effect (creation of the universe).

❖ **Biblical Scripture**: "Do not be deceived: God cannot be mocked. A man reaps what he sows. Whoever sows to please their flesh, from the flesh will reap destruction; whoever sows to please the Spirit, from the Spirit will reap eternal life." – Galatians 6:7-8 (NIV)

❖ **Universal Law Principle:** The Law of Cause-and-Effect states that every action has a reaction; every cause has an effect. This law indicates that nothing happens by chance and that every effect we see in our physical world has a specific cause that originates in the mental or spiritual realm.

## II.	The Law of Biogenesis

❖ **Scientific Principle**: Life arises from existing life rather than non-living matter. This is supported by modern biology and the experiments of Louis Pasteur.

❖ **Biblical Scripture**: "And the Lord God formed man of the dust of the ground, and breathed into his nostrils the breath of life; and man became a living soul" (Genesis 2:7). This can be interpreted as life coming from a living God.

## III.	Conservation of Mass and Energy (First Law of Thermodynamics)

❖ **Scientific Principle**: Matter and energy cannot be created or destroyed, only transformed from one form to another.

❖ **Biblical Scripture**: While not explicitly mentioned, the creation account implies a finite, completed creation which aligns with this principle.

❖ **Universal Law Principle**: Law of Perpetual Transmutation of Energy, Energy is constantly changing forms, but it is never created or destroyed. This law suggests that energy is in constant motion and everything is in a state of flux. Positive energy can be converted into negative energy and vice versa, depending on one's thoughts and actions.

IV.   The Water Cycle

❖ **Scientific Principle**: Water evaporates, forms clouds, and returns as precipitation.

❖ **Biblical Scripture**: "He draws up the drops of water, which distil as rain to the streams; the clouds pour down their moisture and abundant showers fall on mankind" (Job 36:27-28).

❖ **Universal Law Principle**: The Law of Perpetual Transmutation of Energy states that energy is constantly changing forms but is never created or destroyed.

V.   The Spherical Earth

❖ **Scientific Principle**: The Earth is a sphere.

❖ **Biblical Scripture**: "He sits enthroned above the circle of the earth, and its people are like grasshoppers" (Isaiah 40:22). The term "circle" can be interpreted as a reference to the roundness of the Earth. How would they have known this before telescopes?

VI.   Principle of Ship Design: Proportional Dimensions for Stability

❖ **Scientific Principle**: The proportions of a vessel are critical for its stability, buoyancy, and seaworthiness. Modern ship design uses specific ratios to ensure that ships can withstand rough seas without capsizing.

     Unveiling the Gospel Truth Beyond Colonial Shadows

❖ **Biblical Reference**: Genesis 6:15 provides the dimensions of Noah's Ark: "The ark is to be three hundred cubits long, fifty cubits wide and thirty cubits high." These dimensions give a length-to-width ratio of 6:1 and a length-to-height ratio of 10:1.

While scientific laws are based on empirical evidence and testable hypotheses, biblical scriptures are inspired texts conveying spiritual and moral truths. Despite these differences, we still see alignment. One might wonder how the biblical authors could have known such things without being scientists. Considering their backgrounds – such as Paul the tentmaker, Peter the fisherman, Nehemiah the cupbearer to the Persian king, Matthew the tax collector, Amos the shepherd and fig tree farmer, David the shepherd, musician, and poet, and Moses the shepherd boy – it is clear that they were indeed hearing from the God who created the heavens and the earth. How else would they have known such things if they had not been hearing from the same God behind the intelligence of the design?

The same is true when evaluating universal laws, such as the 12 laws of the universe or sometimes seven, depending on the author, the very laws that are deemed to be the very centre of all there is. However, when delving deeper, one can also confirm that they are but the scriptures. This aligns with the principle of empirical evidence, which suggests that for a hypothesis to be valid, it should be repeatable. Therefore, the observers who formulated these laws did nothing special other than observing the pattern behind the design.

The renowned scientist Isaac Newton, one of the most influential figures in history known for his work in physics, mathematics, and astronomy, believed that the Bible contained valuable knowledge and insights that could aid in scientific understanding and research. He once said that if the world could come to this realisation, they would embrace the God of the Bible.

11.6 Biblical Nuggets Relevant to Day-to-Day Life: Success, Relationships, Health, Personal Growth, and Unity

When engaging with the biblical text within the correct and intended context, you will find it empowering. There is never anything detrimental to the reader, for it is written for teaching, empowering, rebuking, correcting, and training. The scripture 2 Timothy 3:16-17 (NIV) reads, "All Scripture is God-breathed and is useful for teaching, rebuking, correcting and training in righteousness, so that the servant of God may be thoroughly equipped for every good work." The Word of God provides timeless wisdom and principles that are applicable to modern life, for success, relationships, health, personal growth for the benefit of everyone who read it (no racism). Below are some examples:

1.   **Confidence and Self-Actualisation**

   "I can do all things through Christ who strengthens me." – Philippians 4:13 (NKJV)

   This verse instils confidence and assurance in one's abilities through the strength that comes from Christ. It encourages believers to face challenges with faith in God's empowering grace.

   "For God gave us a spirit not of fear but of power and love and self-control." – 2 Timothy 1:7 (ESV)

   This scripture underscores the courage and confidence that believers receive from God's Spirit. It emphasises the virtues of power, love, and self-control as foundational elements for overcoming fear and living boldly.

   "The fear of man brings a snare, but whoever trusts in the Lord shall be safe." – Proverbs 29:25 (NKJV)

   This encourages reliance on God rather than fear of human opinion or circumstances, fostering inner strength and confidence.

     Unveiling the Gospel Truth Beyond Colonial Shadows

2. **Unity and Equality in Christ**

   "There is neither Jew nor Gentile, neither slave nor free, nor is there male and female, for you are all one in Christ Jesus." – Galatians 3:28 (NIV)

   This verse emphasises the unity and equality of all believers in Christ, transcending race, cultural, social, and gender distinctions.

3. **Teamwork and Collaboration**

   "As iron sharpens iron, so one person sharpens another." – Proverbs 27:17 (NIV)

   This encourages mutual encouragement, growth through collaboration, and the benefits of teamwork.

   "Plans fail for lack of counsel, but with many advisers they succeed." – Proverbs 15:22 (NIV)

   This emphasises the value of seeking wise counsel, teamwork, and collective decision-making.

4. **Psychology and Emotional Intelligence**

   "The wise in heart accept commands, but a chattering fool comes to ruin." – Proverbs 10:8 (NIV)

   This verse encourages wisdom in receiving guidance and discernment in interpersonal relationships.

   "Mockers resent correction, so they avoid the wise." – Proverbs 15:12 (NIV)

   This highlights the importance of humility and openness to feedback for personal growth and emotional intelligence.

5.   Management of Finances, Wealth and Investments

"The rich rule over the poor, and the borrower is slave to the lender." – Proverbs 22:7 (NIV)

This verse highlights the consequences of indebtedness and the importance of financial prudence. It encourages responsible financial management and warns against the risks of indebtedness.

"Ship your grain across the sea; after many days you may receive a return. Invest in seven ventures, yes, in eight; you do not know what disaster may come upon the land."
- Ecclesiastes 11:1-2 (NIV)

These verses advise diversification in investments and business ventures as a strategy for mitigating risks and maximising returns. They emphasise wisdom in financial planning and preparedness for unforeseen circumstances.

"The plans of the diligent lead to profit as surely as haste leads to poverty." – Proverbs 21:5 (NIV)

This verse encourages careful planning, diligence, and strategic thinking in financial matters.

6.   **Moderation in Eating and Drinking**

"Do not join those who drink too much wine or gorge themselves on meat, for drunkards and gluttons become poor, and drowsiness clothes them in rags." – Proverbs 23:20-21 (NIV)

This encourages moderation in food and drink consumption for physical health and financial stewardship.

11.6. Near Death Experiences (NDE)

Near-death experiences can serve as compelling evidence that affirms the authenticity of the message conveyed in the Bible. These experiences have long fascinated and intrigued many, providing glimpses into a realm beyond our earthly existence. Such encounters, often reported by individuals who've faced death and returned, have sparked debates and lured others to commit their lives to investigate this subject.

A striking aspect of near-death experiences is their remarkable consistency, even among people from diverse cultures, belief systems, and religious or cultural backgrounds. People frequently recount similar elements, including feelings of peace and tranquillity, a sense of leaving the physical body, passages through tunnels, encounters with light, gardens, life reviews, the Book of Life, meetings with deceased loved ones or spiritual entities, angels, and sometimes Jesus Christ.

A well-known NDE researcher, David Suich, initially approached the subject with scepticism. However, he ultimately confirmed its genuineness after devoting approximately 14 years to researching this topic. He often expressed astonishment at the striking similarities of what witnesses reported from the other side, particularly the emphasis on love as the paramount aspect emphasised by Jesus or what some refer to as a being of light. There are many more NDE researchers who have even published material on the subject, and their work is widely available.

The message of love as paramount and as the reason for living resonates deeply with the commandment of Jesus found in John 13:34-35, wherein He instructs His followers to love one another: "A new command I give you: Love one another. As I have loved you, so you must love one another. By this everyone will know that you are my disciples, if you love one another." These shared features resonate strongly with the teachings of the Bible. The Bible, a spiritual guide, emphasises love, forgiveness, and purposeful living. For those fortunate enough to experience them, near-death experiences hold profound significance. Some individuals have even glimpsed the revered "Book of Life," a testament to their deeds and faith.

What really astonished me is the testimony of a brother to our family friend who repeatedly told the family that he felt as though his soul was leaving his body. Our friend mobilised prayers across the country. We were also called on for prayers, asking the Lord to have mercy on him and rebuking any dark spirits that may have been responsible. To our surprise, after a brief glimpse into the other realm, he came back to testify. He told us about the experiences he had, including those responsible for his condition and those who prayed, detailing where they were prayed and the clothes they wore.

Others have taken guided tours through heaven and hell, witnessing the celestial beauty of heavenly realms and the darkness of spiritual separation. A notable similarity emerges from these accounts: a sudden repentance and acceptance of the Lord Jesus Christ. In the presence of heavenly glory, individuals undergo profound transformations. Overwhelmed by their imperfections and the consequences of their actions, they experience a radical change of heart, embracing Jesus as their Saviour.

11.7 A Comparative Exploration of Christianity Over Other Religions, and Debunking the Big Bang Theory.

We cannot close the debate or draw conclusions before conducting a comparative exploration of the Gospel of Jesus Christ, or Christianity, in comparison to other religions and famous theories such as the Big Bang theory. It is important to note that they cannot all be true; one must be true, or the others must be false, or all are false. I will also delve into the claim that the Bible was plagiarised from other spiritual traditions or religions, as some assert.

11.7.1. Refuting the Big Bang and Evolution Theory Over the Biblical Creation Account

The debate between the Big Bang and evolution theory versus the biblical creation account has persisted for an extended period. Within this discourse, a faction of individuals opposes the traditional creation narrative, considering the Big Bang as a plausible alternative. It is evident that both cannot be simultaneously true; either both are false, or one is true. This chapter seeks to explore and establish the veracity of each perspective.

In the exploration of the biblical creation narrative, significant efforts have been undertaken to provide tangible evidence aligning with the accounts found in the Bible. A notable example is the work conducted by The Creation Evidence Museum of Texas, formerly known as the Creation Evidence Museum. Located in Glen Rose, Somervell County, central Texas, this creationist museum was established in 1984 by Carl Baugh with the primary objective of researching and showcasing exhibits that substantiate creationism.

What adds intrigue to this pursuit is the growing acknowledgement of the narrative by scientists themselves. Even within scientific circles, there is an emerging recognition of the credibility of aspects presented in the biblical account of creation. In the interest of brevity, I direct the reader to the works available for more comprehensive details and references, in conjunction with the content presented in the Bible. It's crucial to acknowledge that the subject matter at hand is expansive enough to warrant a book on its own. Hence, the most suitable approach, concerning this topic, is to guide you towards reputable materials for a deeper exploration.

When it comes to the Big Bang and evolution theory, I always appreciate the submissions of Mar Mari Emmanuel, the Bishop of Christ the Good Shepherd Church, on this topic. He expressed that evolution stems from members of the round table — non-believers in God, atheists attempting to find reasons to avoid the idea of one divine Creator responsible for all living things.

Let's consider the notion that everything came into existence because something exploded 13 billion years ago. It's important to note that science remains a theory, subject to mutation over time as we continually discover more information. In contrast, the Bible, on the other hand, is definitive in its propositions. Logically, let's entertain the idea that this intricately designed universe came into existence due to an explosion. Is it not akin to stating that the Oxford Dictionary or the laptop you use daily just happened to appear coincidentally after something exploded? Would that make sense to you at all? When you think of the Oxford Dictionary or a laptop, you immediately think of the intelligent brain behind it, right? Now, what about the universe, which is more complex than the Oxford Dictionary and the laptop?

Allow me to provide an example of human DNA. Human DNA is said to be made of 3.1 billion bits of information. If we were to convert that into words and write them on an A4 paper, with 500 words per page, we would use 600,000 pages to write one person's DNA; how could that just happen coincidentally or as a result of an incident? Currently, there are about 7.9 billion people living on this planet as of 2024, each with different fingerprints that have never been duplicated since the beginning of creation. Are they expecting us to believe that an explosion can create such an intelligent system?

Even within the confines of scientific scrutiny, the Big Bang and evolution theory fails to align with established scientific principles. The notion that a man could emerge from a unicellular organism is fundamentally flawed. In terms of evolution, we understand that the process cannot be incremental. This means that acquiring new

   Unveiling the Gospel Truth Beyond Colonial Shadows

information in your DNA is not a spontaneous occurrence; rather, the information should have been pre-encoded, undergoing mutations to adapt to new environmental conditions.

Examining the concept of a unicellular organism evolving into the intricate complexity of a human being becomes an implausible phenomenon. The intricacies of such a transformation raise questions about the feasibility of such evolutionary leaps, challenging the very core of the proposed evolutionary model.

Someone might counter-question by asking, "Who created God then, if nothing comes from nothing?" My response to that debate is that if we knew who created God, or if He needed to be created, or if our minds could comprehend Him, that would immediately disqualify Him as God. We understand that for a creator to have the capability to bring forth the universe, they must exist outside of it. Research has revealed that for a being to create the universe, they must transcend space and time – a description that aligns with the God of the Bible.

11.7.2. The Spiritual Superiority of Christ Over Other Gods

In the ongoing struggle among various power sources, a consistent principle emerges: the stronger force will always assert dominance over the weaker. This fundamental truth echoes throughout history, resonating across all realms and dimensions. Nowhere is this principle more vividly illustrated than in the unparalleled confrontation between the potency of Jesus Christ and the malevolent forces allied with Satan – sorcerers, false religions, psychics, and those dwelling in the obscure realms of darkness.

I grew up in a family where both my parents were believers in the name of the Lord Jesus Christ. My late father served as an Apostle of God, called to the ministry of healing, deliverance, and miracles. Thus, I was fortunate to witness these experiences from a very tender age, observing the dominance that the name of the Lord Jesus Christ held over others. This is the same power I continue to witness daily in my life, as detailed in the chapter recounting my personal encounters. The name of Jesus dominates all others, just as it is written in the scriptures that every knee shall bow, and every tongue confess that Jesus Christ is the Lord. This includes the names of false gods from other religions, an experience we witness daily.

I also mentioned that my grandfather was a witch doctor and a spiritualist, an authentic practitioner who used to manipulate events at our site. However, on the day he passed away, he called on my father to lead him to salvation, acknowledging that he already knew Jesus Christ as the only way. He had kept his subscription to his practices for survival purposes.

In the spiritual realm, the name of Jesus Christ holds unparalleled authority. His power, derived from divine sources, encompasses boundless strength fuelled by love, compassion, and unwavering faith. The name of Jesus Christ symbolises hope, salvation, and the driving force behind miracles.

In contrast, within the depths of darkness reside those who harness malevolent powers – the agents of Satan, practitioners of dark arts, and wielders of forbidden knowledge. They manipulate the realms of the occult, seeking to bend reality to their will and conspiring to disrupt the divine order. However, despite their cunning and deceit, their power is a flickering candle compared to the radiant sun.

When the forces of light and darkness collide, powers of evil might put up temporary resistance, invoking illusions of opulence and deceptive displays of strength. However, their power, hidden in shadows, cannot compare to the radiance of divine authority. Just as night inevitably gives way to dawn, the forces aligned with darkness submit to the power of Jesus Christ.

This phenomenon is observable both within church gatherings and in any assembly convened in the name of the Lord Jesus Christ. Even the agents of darkness dispatched to disrupt such gatherings find

    Unveiling the Gospel Truth Beyond Colonial Shadows

themselves subdued under the authority of Jesus Christ's name. This phenomenon is also evident during exorcisms, healings, and during prayers for those grappling with psychological or other challenges. The name of the Lord Jesus Christ consistently triumphs. This is a reality rarely seen in other religions worldwide. Even those from other faiths can attest that they find complete peace after encountering the peace and freedom found only in the name of the Lord Jesus Christ.

We also witness those who were once entrenched in Satanism testifying about the power of Jesus Christ and the havoc it wreaks in the kingdom of darkness compared to other religions. For those seeking more details, I gladly refer you to a documentary available on YouTube, presented by Erica, a former Satanist and devil worshipper who was fortunately delivered by the power in the name of Jesus Christ. Her YouTube channel is titled "Life is Spiritual." She has also written books on this subject, which are available on her website: https://www.lifeisspiritual.org/.

11.7.3. Examining the Claim of the Bible's Plagiarism from Other Spiritual Traditions

One thing we can all agree on, at least, is that the spiritual realm is as real as the physical realm. Just as there are laws governing the physical world, there are laws that govern the spiritual realm. Therefore, it shouldn't be surprising to find parallels between Christianity and other spiritualities or religions. People who have been involved in satanism, occultism, or other deep spiritual practices often testify that, just as Christians fast to enhance their spiritual sharpness, similar practices exist in the kingdom of Satan. Laws are universal, regardless of the kingdom they belong to, which also explains why their writings might mimic holy scriptures to some extent. For instance, in Christianity, we speak of the blood of Jesus as a sacrifice for our sins to God the Father, while in satanism, occultism, or other deep spiritual practices, they may speak of sacrificing humans to appease their masters. However, the crucial difference lies in the spirit behind these operations, which is why the Bible encourages us to test the spirits, as there can be many counterfeits. As I mentioned above in the section titled "The Spiritual Superiority of Christ Over Other gods", we have repeatedly witnessed that in any confrontation between the kingdom of God and other spirits, the other spirits always surrender. Additionally, what God gives is permanent, while the enemy's provisions are temporary and come with punishment and eventual destruction. Proverbs 10:22 teaches that "The blessing of the Lord makes rich, and he adds no sorrow with it." In John 10:10, we learn that "The thief comes only to steal and kill and destroy; I have come that they may have life and have it to the full." Thus, the gospel of the Lord Jesus Christ revolves around love, while the enemy is about deception and malice.

I also need to clarify a common confusion between culture and spirituality. Many Africans defend what they refer to as African spirituality, confusing it with their culture. It's important to understand that culture refers to the way of life developed by a group of people to manage their interactions, while spirituality is the way of connecting with the divine or deity. There is absolutely nothing wrong with most cultural practices; many can even be traced back to the Torah, as explained in previous chapters. However, what is often referred to as African spirituality is actually satanic when we examine its practices more closely. As we've discussed, there can only be one true God who is central to everything and everyone, as even science suggests we all came from a single ancestor. If we all came from the same ancestor, we were made by the same God. If there is only one God, then there must be a prescribed way of reaching Him, unlike the conflicting practices we see around us. Did you know that people who can see in the spirit recognise that the Lord Jesus (Yeshua) is the only way to God? I recommend listening to some confessions by demonic spirits during exorcisms or deliverance services. It is interesting how mere carnal people keep debating this. Anyone with the ability to see in the spiritual realm can attest to the fact that there is only one way

   Unveiling the Gospel Truth Beyond Colonial Shadows

to God, and that is through the Cross of Christ, even if they still resist. Majority gets an opportunity to accept the Lord on their sickbed just like my grandfather alluded to in early chapters.

With this, we can boldly refute the misconceptions about the origin of the Bible, with some claiming it was copied from Egyptian (Kemit) and other practices or scriptures. The content of the Bible, which we have already discussed in previous chapters, is supported by consistent historical, archaeological, and textual evidence. Unlike the myths and religious practices of the texts in question, the Bible is a cohesive narrative written by over 40 authors across different continents and over a span of 1,500 years, yet it maintains a unified message. Additionally, we have seen prophecies within the Bible fulfilled accurately, demonstrating its divine inspiration. Furthermore, spiritually, whenever there are confrontations between spirits from different kingdoms, all surrender to the name of the Lord Jesus Christ. The ethical and moral teachings of the Bible further attest to its authenticity as the Word of God.

12

Conclusion

After thorough examination, it becomes clear that the Bible stands as the authentic Word of God, resilient against attempts to discredit its credibility. Despite co-optation by colonial rule and misinterpretation by certain religious institutions discussed in this book, the Bible's core message remains steadfast. Its teachings on love, forgiveness, redemption, liberation, and purpose resonate deeply with humanity's collective consciousness, reflecting divine origin, love of the creator, His holiness, inclusiveness for all mankind, and the justice of God.

Furthermore, the convergence of evidence from diverse disciplines, including scientific discoveries, archaeological findings, and personal testimonies, reinforces the Bible's authenticity. This multidimensional validation underscores its historical accuracy and relevance. Moreover, the Bible's transformative power is undeniable, as countless individuals have experienced spiritual renewal and healing through its message. Its ability to transcend cultural and temporal boundaries, speaking directly to the human heart, affirms its divine origin.

13

The Sinner's Prayer!

efore you drop this book and now that you have been enlight-
ened, I want to take a moment to emphasise the significance
of accepting Jesus Christ into your life through the sinner's prayer.
There is God, Jesus, the Holy Spirit, Satan, Angels, Heaven, and Hell,
and life after death. Jesus died for our sins so that we can be recon-
ciled with the Father after the fall of Adam in the Garden of Eden.
It is important to note that the sinner's prayer is not merely a ritual
or formality; it is a profound step towards a transformative relationship with God. Accepting Jesus as your Saviour is pivotal because it
acknowledges your need for redemption and forgiveness. Through
the sinner's prayer, we express our faith in Jesus' sacrifice for our sins
and invite Him to be our Lord. Romans 10:9 teaches us that if you
declare with your mouth, "Jesus is Lord," and believe in your heart
that God raised Him from the dead, you will be saved. Romans 10:10
teaches us that you believe and are justify with your heart, and with
your mouth you profess your faith and you are saved.

It's a decision that has eternal implications, shaping not only your
present but also your afterlife. So, when praying, we need to mean
it and genuinely believe in our hearts; this cannot be forced into
anyone as it must happened wilfully. So, if you have not accepted the
Lord Jesus Christ yet, please read the prayer below from the heart,
and you shall be saved.

Please repeat the following prayer after me, understanding its significance:

"Dear Lord Jesus, I come before You acknowledging that I am a sinner in need of Your forgiveness. I believe that You are the Son of God, who came to earth, died on the cross for my sins, and rose again. I repent of my sins and ask for Your mercy and grace to cleanse me. I invite You into my heart to be my Lord and Saviour, guiding my life from this moment forward. Help me to walk in Your ways and to live according to Your Word. Thank you for welcoming me into Your family. In Jesus' name, Amen."

By sincerely praying this prayer, you have taken the first step towards a new life in Christ. It is important to seek guidance from a local church or fellow believers to grow in your faith and nurture your relationship with God. Remember, the key is not only to accept Christ but also to strive to live a life that aligns with His teachings.

 Unveiling the Gospel Truth Beyond Colonial Shadows

References

a)   Hammer, M. F., Redd, A. J., Wood, E. T., et al. (2000). "Jewish and Middle Eastern non-Jewish populations share a common pool of Y-chromosome biallelic haplotypes." Proceedings of the National Academy of Sciences, 97(12), 6769-6774.

b)   Diop, Cheikh Anta. (1974). "The African Origin of Civilization: Myth or Reality." Lawrence Hill Books.

c)   Parfitt, Tudor. (2013). "Black Jews in Africa and the Americas."

d)   Rabbi Jonathan Bernis. YouTube Channel: "Jewish Voice." Retrieved from [URL: https://www.youtube.com/channel/UC9Y0TYBGxEbrjEFigFldIvw].

e)   The Holy Bible: English Standard Version. Crossway, 2001

f)   NIV the New International Version

g)   New King James Version (NKJV)

h)   A Ready Defense: The Best of Josh McDowell Paperback – September 1, 1992

i)   A Strong Faith Ministries – YouTube, [URL: https://youtu.be/HOWTqRfm-Co?si=lzKYBsoOmnmqt6lg]

j)   "Heavens Awaits – Near Death Experience."
YouTube, [URL: https://www.youtube.com/channel/
UCJ6ecjeynuslt_RvpYw9o7Q]

k)   Luonde. "Vhavenda History." [URL: https://luonde.co.za/]

l)   Montagu, Ashley. (1942). "Man's Most Dangerous Myth: The
Fallacy of Race." Columbia University Press.